BEARS AND MEN

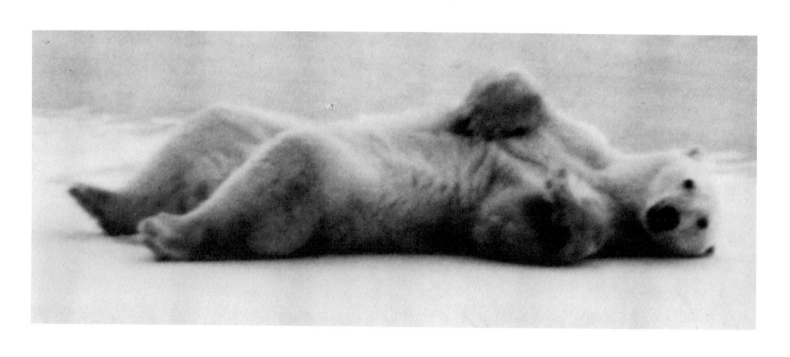

Algonquin Books of Chapel Hill

1986

William Mills

BEARS AND MEN

A Gathering

Also by William Mills

Watch for the Fox: Poems

I Know a Place: Stories

Louisiana Cajuns
(introductory text)

Stained Glass: Poems

*The Stillness in Moving Things:
The World of Howard Nemerov*

The Meaning of Coyotes: Poems

Those Who Blink: A Novel

published by
Algonquin Books of Chapel Hill
Post Office Box 2225, Chapel Hill, North Carolina 27515-2225
in association with
Taylor Publishing Company
1550 West Mockingbird Lane, Dallas, Texas 75235

Library of Congress Cataloging-in-Publication Data

Mills, William, 1935–
Bears and men.

Bibliography: p.
1. Polar bear. 2. Churchill Region (Manitoba)—
Description and travel. 3. Mammals—Manitoba—
Churchill Region. I. Title.
QL737.C27M54 1986   917.124'1   86–7855
ISBN 0–912697–41–5

An excerpt from *Bears and Men: A Gathering* first
appeared in the *New Virginia Review Anthology 4.*

Mills's poems "Rock, Snow, Bear, Sky" and "Lords"
first appeared in his *The Meaning of Coyotes* (LSU Press,
1986).

for Beverly

BEARS AND MEN

Rock, Snow, Bear, Sky

The bears are mounds of white
In the arctic night,
The foxes move silently,
Their tails settled with soft snow.
The moon is a promise,
The wind sure.

Here
Surrounded by the tundra night
And the best of men
I have by this cold simplicity
Prepared myself for everywhere.

Thirty thousand feet over central Canada is good vantage for sensing the spent power of receding glaciers from the last ice age. Small ponds and lakes pock the taiga below us, gouged by the ice that had abandoned the land long ago. My two new companions and I on this six-hundred-mile flight from Winnipeg to Churchill were gathering with several other men for a photographic expedition to Cape Churchill. For polar bears.

The previous summer I had lunched with the photographer Dan Guravich, while he was in Louisiana to discuss with his publisher a book he planned to bring out on the brown pelicans. During the course of our first meeting, he suggested I come along on a little expedition to observe and photograph the polar bears of Hudson Bay. He explained that for several years he had pursued them and that Cape Churchill had proved to be the ideal site. In the thick heat of that subtropical summer day, the thought of snow was singularly appealing; the possibility of seeing polar bears outside of zoos was magnetic.

For nearly everyone bears are magical animals. They often accompany us as we begin our lives, in the form of stuffed effigies that we cling to for emotional support, their size commensurate with our own amidst the towering figures we come to call adults.

Shortly thereafter we are enthralled by a rather forward, golden-locked little girl who moves in on the living quarters of three bears and makes herself right at home. And after another spurt of time, at least in the United States, we find ourselves being instructed by a giant, friendly bear on highway signs about proper manners in the forest. After confronting the likes of Goldilocks, it's no wonder Smoky felt the need to improve our etiquette.

My only childhood brush with a real bear had been with a black one in the Smoky Mountains. I awoke during the night to see a dark figure looming over my cot and mosquito bar. So help me, he said, "Woof." Exactly how I managed to escape to my parents' larger tent I will never know. The next morning an old, light-green Dr. Pepper cooler in which my mother kept the bacon and eggs for our breakfast had been twisted into a corkscrew. Until that same trip I believed I could surely outrun a bear (they seemed to move sluggishly or else dawdled in the trees of my books), even though I might have to run barefooted to do it, doing Mercury one better.

Smoky the Bear, my bear leader (in German, *Bärenführer*), would soon turn me over to the bear of our greatest novelist, Faulkner. And there the mighty animal's magic would swell to fit an expanding universe.

The several men who were now gathering for this photographic expedition had likewise been strong incentive for the trip. At first there were to be three others besides Guravich and myself (along with two local Churchill men, Len Smith and Roy Bukowsky). On the plane were Fred Treul and Harry Albers. Treul was an industrialist from Milwaukee who had been to Churchill the previous summer. Of Austrian ancestry, he was in his fifties and wore his graying hair pulled straight back in European fashion. An avid amateur photographer, Treul had been photographing some of the thousands of nesting birds during the summer.

Harry Albers, an eminent veterinary surgeon, had a national reputation for giving his time to mend broken birds and animals for the Sun Coast Seabird Sanctuary. Guravich had met Albers while photographing the brown pelicans at the sanctuary and had urged him to leave the balmy Gulf Coast for the 10°F that met us when we landed in Churchill. It was to get colder.

The only other member of the initial group was Fred Bruemmer, who had arrived a couple of days early, along with Guravich. Bruemmer's home base was Montreal but from all accounts, he spent half his time traveling the Arctic.

We were greeted at the small airfield in Churchill by Joe Kowal, owner of the Polar Motel. Exactly how one might "motor" up to a motel in Churchill was never made clear. There are no roads to Churchill. Only tracks for Canadian ViaRail. But travelers are grateful for any accommodations where almost everything from lumber to limburger cheese must be shipped in.

Joe, a stocky fellow, was wearing a cap that said "I Am a Fox Hunter." Growing up in Mississippi and Louisiana, I had sat around fires listening to hounds scream through the night, and I immediately figured he was of this breed. Straight out of the chute I said, "You're a fox hunter, huh?"

Momentarily he forgot he had this information on his hat and looked at me suspiciously, almost accusingly.

"I didn't expect to run into a fox hunter way up here. Hounds must have a rough time."

He grinned when I said this. "No, no. We trap them."

Later I would learn why Joe had seemed defensive. Some of his customers, here to photograph the nesting birds in summer or the bears in winter, object strenuously to trapping and have told him as much. But whether he makes part of his living trapping or not, he doesn't fake it when he's around tourists reared in large cities. His cap, if not his panache, is a declaration, so that the matter can be aired or passed over straightaway.

We put duffel bags and camera gear in the back of his pickup for the ride into town. The bed of the truck was covered with ice and snow. The 737 that had brought us in was being refueled while Indians, Eskimos, locals from Churchill, and other seekers of the bear, prepared for the trip back to Winnipeg. Along the several miles into town we could see Hudson Bay to the east, loaded with ice but not frozen over. To the left was a frozen tidal backwater of the Churchill River. The land was flat to the west, but straggles of black spruce were evident. And though the snow was a couple of feet deep, the endurable willows humped their load and endured. As we approached the Bay's coast, the tundra gave way to granite that rose as if to hold back the lashes of winter's waves. Atop the rocks was a gigantic research windmill, underwritten by the Canadians to discover how much of this wind power could be converted to usable electricity.

The little town of Churchill in winter is mostly mounds of snow one story high. There is the old railroad station that marks the end of the one thousand *land* miles back to Winnipeg. At the far end of town, near the mouth of the river, is the most imposing structure—the grain elevators. Since the distance to many European ports is shorter from Churchill than from the Great Lakes and the St. Lawrence River, there were high hopes for shipping a lot of the grain from the prairie provinces. Shipping has declined of late, however, and of course the ice-free shipping season is always very brief.

Churchill's most surprising complex of buildings is its Community Center and hospital. Near numerous ramshackled residences, the Center, which cost millions, is of very contemporary architecture. The hospital serves thousands of square miles of the central Arctic, and emergencies from distant tiny villages are "medivaced," or flown in, for the only available help. A couple of blocks away, someone has four husky sled dogs on their chains.

Europeans settled Churchill in the 1680s because of the numerous beluga whales that come every summer. Like so many other towns in Canada, Churchill began when the Hudson's Bay Company (HBC) established a small trading post. From there it shipped casks of whale oil back to England. Across the river from where we are stand the huge remains of Fort Prince of Wales. The HBC began construction on this much larger facility in 1733 and finished it in 1771. It was from the walls of this fort that Samuel Hearne, the explorer (and later governor of it), left to walk to the Arctic Ocean. The whales still come every summer, and some of them are captured by locals for zoos around the world. No one visits the fort during winter. From a distance its November desolation hints of what its winter would have been like two hundred years ago.

At our one-story motel, essentially a long hall with rooms, I drew Harry Albers as roommate. There was even television. An Alabama-Georgia football game was playing and I asked why folks near 59°N would choose this over Canadian sports. I got my explanation. Ted Turner's satellite network was being ripped off and piped into the houses.

Guravich announced there would be several others joining the trip, two of whom were policemen! That was a shock and a little disconcerting at the time. For the first night, though, only five of us gathered for dinner. One of the eateries had some arctic char, which rarely reaches the United States. I know of no better-tasting fish. And unless you get it fresh out of the frigid waters of the local rivers in summer, it is likely flash frozen and flown in from Eskimo camps further up the coast, left then to dry out in freezers. Yet it survives all of this, still possessing a delicate richness as it is broiled in butter. Eskimos have it another way. They dry it on racks in the open air, cross-hatching it to keep the fish bodies from curling. Once the fish is dry, the Eskimos pass by occasionally and cut off a piece.

I looked forward to meeting Fred Bruemmer with great anticipation. He was not only a well-known Arctic nature photographer, he was a writer as well. I had not come unprepared. For a month or so before I arrived in Churchill I had been reading, and much of the time was spent with Bruemmer's books—those that I could get. I had borrowed the only one Guravich had, *The Arctic,* and had rummaged for three others. The public library in Baton Rouge had *Encounters with Arctic Animals* and *Seasons of the Eskimo.* And I finally got *The Long Journey* through interlibrary loan from somewhere in Illinois.

All the dust jackets said about him was that he was a German-speaking Latvian who had come to Canada in 1950. He began working in the mines of Kirkland Lake in northern Ontario and took up photography because "when you don't know the language it's good to learn photography." He was subsequently awarded the Order of Canada for his polar bear photography.

I first saw him in the room he would be sharing with Guravich for the two nights before we left Churchill. A slender man in his early fifties, he was not at all muscular in the way you might anticipate for a man who has spent large parts of every year for a quarter of a century all over the Arctic. His high-domed forehead and baldness suggested more a European intellectual. His long, slim fingers held one cigarette after another.

At dinner that first evening the subject of pollution came up, a subject that comes up frequently and sadly among people from the industrial countries who spend time in the out-of-doors. Bruemmer was talking about lichens in the Arctic, hardly a place of intense industrialization. "Lichens have been found to absorb strontium 90 and cesium 137 from the atmosphere, a result of atomic explosions. The caribou eat the lichens, their principal food, and concentrate these substances; the Eskimos, in turn, kill and eat the caribou. Eskimos have been found to be contaminated at levels considered barely 'safe.'"

Guravich brought up his summer of photographing the brown

pelican along the Gulf Coast, especially in Florida, and began talking about what Harry was encountering in his work with wounded pelicans in the St. Petersburg area, about how pollution in the water enters the food chain. Because there are so many factors to consider in questions like this, the engendering cause is often never discovered.

"The die-off of brown pelicans that we had in St. Petersburg is a case in point," Albers agreed. "Because a loon die-off had been linked by somebody to heavy metal poisoning, soon the newspapers were reporting that the same thing was happening with the pelicans. And I wondered how they knew that."

"Yah, tell 'em what you found, Harry, tell 'em what you found," urged Guravich.

"Most of the birds were found near a municipal dump station that was dumping raw sewage, which attracted a lot of small fry fish. Normally the pelican dives for his food, but in this case they scooped the small fish from the shallow water with their beaks. Then they would sit in the contaminated sediments and preen themselves. The parasites increased, the bacterial infections increased. Finally certain anaerobes, which produce severe enterotoxins, killed the weakened birds. No significant traces of mercury or lead were found." Likely, Harry argued, the sewage had caused the birds to become so weakened by the combined effects of parasites that they became unable to feed in their normal manner.

We chatted about some other difficult-to-figure food chain items, essentially the problems of ecology. Such questions have often led to "jumped" conclusions, because of the heat that an alerted public can bring to bear. Circumstances can at times demand a quick conclusion. And unlike the mistaken view of a young college instructor I once had—"It's wrong to generalize," a silliness I repeated until I came to my senses—most of our chosen actions result from generalization. What the instructor had meant, of course, was "hasty" generalization. But what is hasty for one is languid for another. Are you in jungle combat or forming conclusions about a galaxy a hundred light years away?

We crunched our way back to the Polar Motel, the snow dusting our parkas. Tomorrow we would buy the provisions that were to last us a couple of weeks. Harry and I settled into our room.

Because I had been unable to buy Bruemmer's books where I lived, I had photocopied some of the text of certain ones. I dug out of my duffel those copied pages of *Seasons of the Eskimo*, hoping to discover more about him and his ideas. What intrigued me was the fact that this man spoke no English in 1950 and yet his books revealed the most limpid of styles, with a simplicity that I particularly favored. How did this obtain? Of course I had cut my teeth on the legend of Nabokov: a gentleman who published in Russian for the first half of his career, then turned agilely to English, and became one of our greatest prose stylists. Yet the biography of Nabokov describes a young boy brought up by English-speaking governesses and in a family that, like many other upper-class Russian families, affected things British. He could at least read English before Russian. That may allow us who speak and write it natively to save a little face. What about Joseph Conrad then? Well, there was Ford Madox Ford's help.

My envy only deepened when I learned that Bruemmer picks up the rudiments of a language in six months. For him, *rudiments* means the technical competence of your average native. He knows ten languages: his native German, English, French, Russian, some Eskimo, Spanish, Dutch, Danish, Norwegian, and Polish. He has been a reporter and editor on English-language newspapers in Canada. And, as I was to discover, he has an encyclopedic memory. One night, some wag came up with some off-color questions that could only be answered with the titles of Shakespeare's comedies (e.g., "Love's Labor's Lost," etc.). Bruemmer got all the hard ones. An accent is still there. His trochaic "Oh yeah" echoes the German "Ja ja." So . . . at least a little flaw.

Harry was reading too on this first evening, his magazine held close to his face as he lay in bed. Finally he got up and found a small bottle in his kit. In his pajamas and thick glasses, he reminded me a little of the genial Elmer Fudd of Bugs Bunny fame. Large head and forehead, balding, with long silver hair at the sides.

"I've got glaucoma," he explained. "And I have to put these drops of pilocarpine in every night." After he finished, he lay still for a moment.

"You want the lights out?"

"No, no. I never go to bed at home till one or two. Of course I take a little nap when I can after supper," laughing. He spoke with his eyes closed and it was a bit odd, though not uncomfortable, to carry on a conversation like that. We had really just met.

"The eye doctors tell me as long as I put these drops in, they will generally arrest the disease, so there's no real choice. They're fairly painful, though. Actually, a good bit so. Little blackouts and nausea."

I sometimes think that being one of the lucky folks who's never been struck down in any significant way makes you more vulnerable to the threat that you will be. Your apprehension of disaster seems somehow more undoing, though most of us would never choose to poultice the dreaded pain with the real thing. I imagined the drops burning at Harry's eyeballs and even shuddered. But it turned out this was only a small part of Harry's suffering—a part he had accustomed himself to.

"I don't know if Dan has mentioned it, but I'm going through a divorce right now."

"No, he hadn't mentioned it." And he hadn't.

Harry pursed his lips thoughtfully, his loose facial skin very expressive. He seemed to say with his face what he could not say with his eyes. Laughing quietly, "Yeah, she's in the house by the water . . . I'm in an apartment now. She got the low-mileage Buick, I got the old Olds. Well, I hadn't wanted the house anyway. She and her parents picked it out. I wanted something else, but no go. Next time, I'm going to have something next to the water."

"Yes. Seems a pity to live on the Gulf and not be by the water. Of course everybody can't be next to the water."

"But I moved all the way from Iowa for the sun and the sand. I'll never forget. I was trying to pull a calf out of a heifer who was having trouble. It was snowing and sleeting and there was ice in the water troughs. But after years in the cornfields of home, I decided I'd had enough. You know the family farm is there still. I had another farm, but my wife's lawyers have decided that it would be just about the right swap for me to have joint custody of my son."

"Jesus, ain't love grand. Well, if it's any consolation, which I know it won't be, I went through a divorce myself, some years ago. It's like passing kidney stones: if you'd known what the pain was going to be like, you might not have had them to start with."

"You, too, huh?" He brightened a little, like maybe I had slipped him the sign of the Masons or something, but of the lodge of the divorced, the failed.

"Kids?"

"No."

"That's probably for the best. My wife couldn't have any so we adopted a son. Actually it's him I'm going to miss. We waited, you know, awhile before we got married. I was in my thirties." Harry seemed to be in his midfifties now.

Our intimacies went on until the wee hours. Funny how it's sometimes easier to share the closest-kept pains and secrets with a stranger. It's like the plan to rocket all our radioactive waste into deep space. Out of sight, out of mind. Yet there is an easy familiarity that doesn't staunch the flow between one and the other, before calluses and scar tissue make it harder to feel.

2

There is something distinctly mind-opening about being confronted with inordinate increments of what one eats, wears, or uses to clean himself. Like all the socks he will wear out in a lifetime, a thousand tubes of toothpaste, or bars of soap. Thought of that way, without the full quotient of lifetime consumables, the proportion of our precious, finite time on the planet that we spend brushing and scrubbing seems excessive. So it was in the Hudson's Bay Company store, called simply "the Bay" by Canadians. We trooped in, filling first one shopping cart, then another, until each of us had at least one magnificent load. Our supply was impressive even for the outlanders who lived by Goose Creek, eight miles away, and sometimes couldn't get into town for food.

I must say, the inside of the Bay was a bit of a letdown from the fantasies I had brought with me in tales of colonial Canada. I had expected to see animal pelts hanging from the ceiling, steel traps and snowshoes, maybe even a dog sled or two. Wrong. Instead I was met with your average chain grocery store, combined with a variety store for cloth material, pots and pans, and the like. All at double the standard prices, because it had to come the thousand land miles from Winnipeg.

Guravich most of all seemed to revel in the shopping spree. It was he who turned out to be the cook for our expedition. "How much cheddar, how much cheddar? Fred, Fred?" Both Treul and Bruemmer turned around. "How much cheese can you eat? Half a pound a day?"

Treul: "I don't eat that much cheese in a week."

"Better be safe. Better get a half-pound apiece a day. Let's see . . . that's seventy pounds! Good grief! Maybe just a third of a pound. . . . Say forty-five pounds." And so it went. Sixty pounds of chicken, sixty of ground beef, sixty of stew meat, a boxcar of spaghetti, and all the bread the Bay had—which set off some grumbling among the other customers. One cart held thirty-five dozen eggs (just thirty a day).

"I need three lemons," I chimed in.

"What d'ya need that for?"

"I need one slice of peel a day for my martinis."

"Bunch of dwunks. Get three dozen. Somebody might need it for their tea."

Len Smith walked up about this time, having parked the truck that would transport all this to the Tundra Buggy. "That reminds me. We got to get liquor." In Canada, there's none in the grocery stores.

"Bunch of dwunks." Guravich's slight speech impediment gives him trouble with his own name. On the phone when he's introducing himself he immediately spells Guravich, too long having had secretaries of company clients ask him to repeat it.

"Better get some mixes here, though," said Smith, ignoring Guravich; he heaps quarts of tomato juice and orange juice into the caravan of carts and turns to me. "You drink Caesars?" I had never heard of them. "Never had a Caesar? Really? Well, we better see to that." A *case* of quarts of the requisite clamato juice.

"How much Red River Cereal?" asked Guravich, addressing the group.

"None for me," replied Smith.

"What is it?" I asked.

"I used to eat it every morning as a kid," replied Guravich. He grew up in Winnipeg. Lots of boxes of Red River Cereal cascade into a separate cart.

Seems like our bill was close to two thousand dollars. The checkout clerk was torn between annoyance at the work and awe at the flood of dollar bills for stuffing the register.

Len Smith—creator of the Tundra Buggy—is the kind of guy that always annoyed me in high school days. You'd be having trouble with getting your '36 Ford started; the skirts were gleaming, the tire kit on the back was dazzling, the dual exhaust pipes were all ready to pulse mellow "dum-dum-dum's"—but the thing wouldn't start. And some character like Len would stroll up, unscrew your air cleaner without asking or being asked, shake the butterfly loose in the carburetor, and of course it started right up. Some have that magic and some don't. At least as an adult Len doesn't show off. But he is one of those that just *has* it: in his hearing, his touch, the overall sensitivity toward an engine that most of us reserve for members of the opposite sex or our children. He's cocky enough to have been like my high school crony, but I wasn't around in southern Manitoba when he was growing up.

When Len's folks had hit Canada from Hungary, they decided to give up the name "Kovac" and landed on what seemed a very popular surname. He has the dark hair and dark eyes that I remember from my own brief time in Budapest. He certified in diesel engine repair and headed to the north country where such skill was worth gold. And he always gives me the impression he could lift the front end of one of his trucks with one hand and change the tire with the other. A front tooth is chipped slightly, and I mean to ask how he got it. Although he is eminently pleasant (even with a snootful of liquor), he may have acquired this disposition gradually, being now thirty-seven years old.

Before he became a Shell Oil distributor, he ran a garage. One winter he fell to talking with Guravich about bears. In those days it was very difficult to get off the several roads that extend from Churchill. The Canadians had built a road out to the rocket range to the south (now defunct except for the peacetime launches for aurora research), and there were several gravel ones off from that. But unless you had something equivalent to an army track vehicle or the kind used in the oil fields, there was no way to get out onto the tundra. That left you having to wait for the bear that might stroll through town or, more often, would be hanging around the garbage dump. Guravich, like Smith, knew that most of the bears stayed at the Cape, waiting for the Bay to freeze over. That was sixty kilometers away and over difficult tundra terrain.

By the time Guravich came back the following season, Smith had built the machine that was subsequently dubbed the "Tundra Buggy." He had taken the differential from a front-end loader, added it to an E600 Ford truck, along with the transfer case from a two-and-a-half-ton truck. He planted all of this on six-ply tires 1 m wide and 1.5 m high, or almost as tall as a man. It was slow (six miles per hour), but sure. Generally.

Rapidly, word of the Buggy traveled among photographers and other pursuers of the strange and exotic. Now the vehicle is on its way to stardom. National Geographic came out to make a film, "The Polar Bears of Churchill"; CBS did a segment on the Sunday Morning Show; and folks like Peter Matthiessen have taken a ride.

Smith had also built the bunkhouse we used, which was some fourteen feet long, on the confiscated bottom of an army track vehicle. It had no power on its own, and had to be towed by the Tundra Buggy. There was room for only eight bunks, four on each side of a small aisle. By the time all the victuals and liquor were stored—as well as the bottled propane and jerry cans of fresh water—there was little space left for anything more. All else, including ten people, had to be stowed in the Buggy itself. Firewood was stacked on the platform aft.

After the shopping excursion, the rest of this day was free. Some of us strolled over to see a collection of Eskimo artifacts under the care of a Catholic priest. Most of the artifacts had, of course, come from the western coast of the Bay. There was a skin boat and lots of carved ivory, some of polar bears. Unless one was very familiar with Eskimo artifacts, though, he would not have been able to distinguish between what are known as Pre-Dorset and Dorset materials. *Dorset* derives from the archaeologists' practice of using the name of the site of the first "find" of new materials—in this case, Cape Dorset.

The emerging story of man in the Arctic and Subarctic has mostly appeared in this century, and it has been put together chiefly by what is left of his tools. Man isn't imaginable without his tools. In a now often-told story, man's presence on this continent is explained by his passage across the "land bridge" that has occasionally existed between eastern Siberia and Alaska. The land bridge occurred when the water level of the sea was lowered because of the water being taken up in the great ice sheets. Generally solid evidence exists that man was in the region of northern Alaska by 28,000 B.C. and there is a possibility that he was there sooner. Coming over from Asia, these Asians made their way over America. The Eskimo was the last group to come across the bridge, around 3,000 B.C.

Because Churchill is at treeline, whereby one can move from the taiga near town out to the tundra of Cape Churchill, it has been a kind of rough confluence of several cultures in prehistory and after. In today's Churchill there are just a few Eskimos, these having drifted down the coast from places like Eskimo Point, Whale Cove, Coral Harbor, or Southampton Island. (Incidentally, the Eskimos of much of Canada prefer the name *Inuit* of their own language, rather than the English rendering of the Algonquian word for them, *Eskimo,* meaning *raw flesh eaters.* Alaskan Eskimos are, on the other hand, comfortable with the Anglicized word.) Most natives that one sees are Indians, descendants of the much earlier people who first crossed the land bridge.

The appearance of Paleo-Indians along and below the treeline followed the shrinking of the Laurentide ice sheet. It started to shrink around 12,000 B.C., and probably by around 5000 B.C. (maybe much earlier) the central shore of Hudson Bay where we are was then free of ice. The Indians followed the newly available land and altered their technology to fit the game. Caribou was the most important game animal. Thus the Indians came to the land of western Hudson Bay from the south. The group of these Indians known as Crees, who are of the Algonquian-speaking group, occupies land south of Churchill. The other group is the Chipewyans, who have occupied land to the west and are members of the Athabascan-speaking group.

The Eskimos did not disperse to the south after they came to the New World, but apparently moved eastward, or north and east. The tool kit of the people who first came to central Canada is very similar to that of what is now known as the Cape Denbigh Flint complex, after the "naming site," Cape Denbigh on the eastern shore of Norton Sound. Both had prepared cores, microblades, burins, retouched burin spalls, incipient side-notched knives. This tradition of making tools is called the Arctic Small Tool Tradition.

The first Eskimos to arrive on Hudson Bay are called Pre-Dorsets. They were on the northern shores of the Bay by 2000 B.C., and they lived principally on the coast and subsisted mainly on seal and walrus. Besides chipped stone, they made tools out of seal and walrus bone, and from ivory. They also had spears and bows and arrows.

Somewhere around 1000 B.C. the Eskimo culture changed to reflect what is known as Dorset. These people seemed to have given up the bow and arrow, perhaps relying more on the spear and harpoon. Dogs were present in both Dorset and Pre-Dorset, but they were not used to pull sleds. Dorsets ground and polished their stone tools more than did their predecessors.

The Dorset culture flourished for a couple of thousand years, and then around A.D. 1000, the superior Thule technology arrived on the scene and gave the newcomers a competitive advantage. The Thule people could take large whales. They had the sealskin-covered kayak and also the larger, open umiak. They also had sleds drawn by dogs. There is no evidence that the Thule people, with greater numbers and better tools, overcame the Dorset Eskimos by force. The two kinds of settlements coexisted for a couple of hundred years, and it is very likely that the Dorsets were gradually assimilated.

I had prevailed on Joe Kowal to let me tag along when he ran his trapline in the afternoon. This was the early part of the season, which generally yielded the best results, Joe said. Although the price of prime pelts in Winnipeg ranged from $35 (for arctic foxes) up to $230 (for Crosses), Joe claimed he trapped more as a hobby than anything else. He was teaching a couple of young people how to trap.

Because Churchill is where tundra and taiga meet, it is a boon for those interested in wild animals, whether feathered or furred. There are those birds of the taiga, for example, that like brush or trees, as well as the wading and shore birds that nest on the tundra. In summer one can find many kinds of passerines in just the kind of terrain we began to walk. Often Joe had a trap set beneath a short spruce. All spruce are short this close to the end of trees.

"I look for tracks," Joe explained. "Not just a single line when he's only passing through, but where it looks like he meanders or hangs around."

This was the first time since my arrival in Churchill that I was feeling the land. It's profound, the difference in *seeing* the land from a car or truck cab and *walking* it. One wouldn't hear much vehicle noise in Churchill anyway, but several miles from town and on the off-trails, we could hear only the crunch of our boots in the snow. Occasionally Joe would comment, "By golly, the little bugger sprung this one," and then kneel to reset and rebait the trap.

When we shifted to the rocks near the coast, we couldn't see the way we could on the tundra, or even as well as we'd seen on the fringes of taiga. As Joe became involved in resetting a trap he said, "Keep an eye out now," and pointed about ten feet away. Eight- or nine-inch bear tracks in the snow! "He left this alone for some reason."

After Joe passed on this piece of wisdom, every snow-covered boulder seemed to be a dozing bear. I remembered Samuel Johnson's having said, "Depend upon it, sir, when a man knows he is to be hanged in a fortnight, it concentrates the mind wonderfully." This applies to seeing bear tracks, too. Joe had left his rifle in the truck.

"I lose a few baits to the rascals," he cackled.

Although I had not yet seen a polar bear run, I remembered that black bear in the Smoky Mountains, and I figured there was no way we could outrun any bear to Joe's truck. Any numbness from the cold was offset by the sharpened senses fear gives birth to.

Soon we came to a trapped fox, an arctic fox. The white fur was not purely white. "Can't use you, little fellow," he explained. Only one foot was in the trap, the right front, and Joe took the four-foot stick he carried, held it next to the neck and head of the fox and released the jaws of the small steel trap with his foot. At first the animal seemed to feel that the trap was still on. He made no move until Joe shooshed him. Then he limped away across the snow, his forepaw dangling uselessly, gradually beginning to run three-legged. Joe rebaited and reset and we moved on.

The next fox, a silver, set off murmurs of approval from my trapping friend, the price being $140 apiece. Running down the side of the stout stick was a small wire rope which led at the end to a collar of sheet metal. Joe was able to slip the collar over the head and pull on the rope to snug the fox to it, keeping it pinned to the ground. Then he stood on the chest, bouncing very lightly until the animal was lifeless.

Before we finished all the sets, four had been collected: two reds, one silver, and one mature arctic fox. So far this season Joe had taken about forty-five. Fox numbers moved in concert with their food. When the lemmings were plentiful, as they obviously were, then there were lots of fox and snowy owls. When the predators up the food chain, like the snowy owl, increased their numbers, what they ate, like the lemming, decreased. And so on in the dance of life.

3

From the warmth of our rooms, we crunched through the zero air, the dark of the early morning lit by our anticipation, all the staging and loading behind us. For the first time all the members came together. I met Roy Bukowsky, formerly with the Canadian Wildlife Service, now teamed with Len in various enterprises in Churchill. Finally, too, the ritual shaking of hands with the two policemen and another participant, Bob Delareuelle. A vigorous, barrel-chested man in his sixties, Bob had been out on one of Len's day trips. Tourists could go out for a short distance on the tundra, but had to head back early because of the slow-moving Tundra Buggy. When he heard about this extended trip for a couple of weeks, he wanted to come aboard.

The two Mounties, Jerry Anderson and Eric Luke, looked like basketball players, both in the six-four range. Right away, my preformed image of the tobacco-chewing, preliterate deputy began to erode. If someone had said Royal Canadian Mounted Police to an American he might have understood better what to expect. And even though nothing on the trip led me to think that either of these cops could sing like Nelson Eddy or drive a dog team like Sergeant Preston with his Yukon King, at least I would have been more aptly prepared for Jerry and Eric by the RCMP label.

As we moved out in the half-light, the white barrenness of this world stood like a statue. The gouging and scraping of the Pleistocene ice sheet was everywhere apparent. Of course all the small tundra ponds that pocked the land like smallpox were frozen, but not always solidly enough to hold the weight of the Buggy. It was sobering to recall that this land over which we rode had been under perhaps eight-to-ten miles of ice only eight thousand years ago. I pelted Bruemmer with questions about everything I saw.

We sought ridges any time they were going generally in the direction of the Cape, for not only did the Buggy have to make it, there was also the bunkhouse we pulled. Very roughly, the ridges that run east to west are lateral moraines, or otherwise terminal moraines. As the glaciers retreated with the slow warming trend that followed an ice age, the rocks and debris were pulled along, then dumped. The ridges of pebble and rock running roughly north and south are the eskers that result from the streams that meandered underneath the glacier. Even with the giant tires of the Buggy, the "deck" rolled and pitched like a boat, sometimes creating a bit of *mal-de-tundra*. Unlike at sea, though, there were enough flat places to provide a little relief.

Off to the right side, a clear trail of little fox tracks punctuated the snow with the determination of all that must keep their minds on food or perish. Bruemmer explained that eskers provided the higher, sandy habitat that the fox and ground squirrels liked for their burrows. Unlike the low-lying, moist flat areas that froze solid, the eskers provided good material for the winter.

We crossed a large esker near Christmas Lake, then traveled north out of our way along the Gordon Lake esker, trying to miss the dense willows. Finally we had to head back east, rough or not. The road ends at Bird Cove; halfway from there to Cape Churchill was Knight's Hill. Because of the flatness of the tundra, a spot of any slight elevation takes on significance, and it was with some anticipation that we rolled and pitched toward the hill. Not only is it halfway, but it gives a different sense of where one "is," in that he feels related to more things: a coastline, more ice, more willows. Of course this does not always work favorably. For some, seeing more in the galaxy, or even more of the earth from 30,000 feet, can be unsettling, can make him feel more lost than before. But for me, Knight's Hill was comforting, if eccentric. And lo, there I saw my first snowy owl.

Forsaking the advantage of this promontory, the big, white owl beat its exit strongly away, startled by our strange machine. There had obviously been enough lemmings this year to keep him around. When the lemming is extremely scarce, this arctic inhabitant is found way down in the United States, even rarely as far south as Louisiana. Very rarely.

For three or four of us it was a first sighting, and that generates its own excitement. Whether it's a blue-gray gnatcatcher or an alpha predator, I am always awed that his species has traveled this far in time, just as mine has. Its strategy for getting here, for carrying some of the original life stuff this far for this long, is impressive, and creates for me a sense of our being members of the same chemistry club. My admiration is even greater when the creature is small. A tiny bundle of the life stuff has answered all the questions the sun, water, and air put to it. Promotion in this school means you get to come to class next year, and social promotion here means the whole species may come.

Eastward again we picked our way through the shrub tundra, the only vegetation showing, the tough stems and leaves of the willow (at least fifteen species of *Salix*), and some dwarf and shrub birch. Though not able to show off like orchids in the tropics, these willows showed off by merely *being there*. They, too, have answered correctly the questions of sun, water, and air, answered in their own style. Lately it's been discovered that some willows can photosynthesize at 32°F or below! Tundra grass (*Du-*

Sunrise on Hudson Bay

Big male on the shore

Mother and twins

Young bear on an esker

"Old Bones"

Bears in the straw

Making his own skidoo

See no evil

Ménage à trois

"Always clean your paws after eating"

pontia) at even 24°. Of course the willow's growth, like all other plant growth in the Subarctic and Arctic, is slow. There was no photosynthesis going on today. There was also no standing tall like a big pine or redwood tree. It costs too much to invest in a tall stem or trunk. What energy there is has to be spent frugally. Because of the winds that come zooming down through Canada, everything keeps a low profile. Besides the abrasiveness of the blown ice crystals and sand, the wind rapidly evaporates any moisture.

Being in the "reduced" world of the tundra reminds me of the time I lived in Japan. For a couple of years I had had my attention, my focus, redirected by the dimensions of that world. Generally speaking, people were shorter, space was reduced, and people were closer together. Greater attention is paid to detail there, as a rule. Size of course is not the sole cause, but I think attention to detail is part of the Japanese stance. Implements of daily utility take on more artistic importance, and the subtle adjustment of a flower stem in a domestic arrangement gathers significance. I became conscious of these differences only after my troopship arrived in California and I was swept away by the vastness of bridges and buildings, the distances between towns. Only the large gesture can be noticed in a tornado of signs. On the tundra, the tiny footprint of a fox seems an audacious message, as does the persistence of a willow or a lichen. Stoic.

"Hey, hey! Look at those tracks." As if out of nowhere and disappearing into the same, the great paws of a bear had padded along in the soft snow. Our anticipation picked up. Not a bear yet, but confirmation that the bears were still here. And soon, by all accounts, they would leave. The bears found in this region have come off the melted ice in southern Hudson Bay during summer. No longer able to kill their favorite food, the seal, they take what they can find and begin their trek up the southwestern coast of the Bay. Perhaps they will find a dead whale that has washed up on the shore. But the pickings are slim. They nibble on grass. That's one reason the garbage dump outside of Churchill attracts a few of them: the scarcity of grub.

But most of them wait around the Cape, because apparently the ice freezes over here a little sooner than in other neighboring possibilities. Liking seals better than grass or the felicities of Churchill, the bears are gone as soon as the ice will carry them easily. And if the ice had been early, our trip could have been largely for nothing. These tracks were a good omen.

Len was aiming for La Pérouse Bay, hopping around the shoreline to miss the willows. We passed near a remote Canadian Wildlife Service summer research camp where thousands of snow geese spend their nesting season. Here they are banded, counted, observed. After they fly south to the Louisiana Gulf Coast for the winter, the camp is boarded up and the researchers are helicoptered out. Bears had broken into one of the cabins; but there were two holes, which confirmed the joke we'd heard in Churchill about how the bear never comes out where he went in. Immensely inquisitive, tremendously strong, the bears often demolish structures in their search for food. Besides hunting food, however, they have a sense of play that can be destructive simply because of their enormous size and strength. The bears play much like a dog plays with a stick, knowing full well there is nothing to eat there, no master to return it to or keep it from.

Once we were in Hudson Bay, the landscape took on a beautiful, eerie quality. When the tide came in, just as the weather turned cold enough for solid freezing, the water froze for several inches at the top and this ice would fall with the receding tide. The bottom of small, shallow La Pérouse Bay was covered with rocks, and as the ice fell it broke over them, leaving jagged teeth-like eruptions. On its way to becoming solid, this icy skin would grow in thickness, rising and falling until there was no more motion. And that is what our bears would be waiting for.

About an hour before the November sun was to set, we came to the finger of land that is Cape Churchill. This would be our neighborhood for some time. And because it was land's end, its significance was enhanced. Being on a cape or a point only etches the feeling more extravagantly. Due east the nearest land was 550 miles away. Hudson Bay is a misnomer, for it is hardly a bay. Rather, it is an inland sea of some 475,000 square miles.

The fever that drives men to attempt the exploration of outer space must be the one that drove the sea explorers from Europe in their quest for the Northwest Passage. The same fever brought Henry Hudson to this great and mysterious body of water in 1610. Actually Hudson had been near the Atlantic entrance once before, as mate on Captain John Davys' voyage of 1587. Davys had gotten this far the preceding year when he came upon a mysterious and terrifying phenomenon which he named the Furious Overfall. Davys called it thus because as he approached it for the first time, the sea seemed to fall down into a gulf with an overfall, the water moving "with diverse circular motions like whirlpools." Hudson was at the wheel when their ship came upon this overfall in 1587 because the captain had been injured. Before he knew it he was in the powerful current—moving rapidly *west* even though the wind was blowing to the *east*. The captain ordered him to turn back to England. But Hudson would remember it in 1610 when he came shooting through the dangerous ice-ridden passage. He was looking, of course, for the Northwest Passage. What modern sailors know is that this great current was the tide being forced through the relatively narrow 100-mile-wide corridor—later named Hudson Strait—between the Atlantic Ocean and Hudson Bay.

Hudson made his way down the eastern coast of the Bay, coming ultimately to James Bay, where he spent a very difficult winter. He was checking for a possible southern outlet before turning to the western coast, but after a point he realized it was too late to sail back out. Because of the scarcity of food, and because he had left England with several scurrilous crewmen, by springtime Hudson and his men were at the breaking point. The mutineers put Hudson, his son John, and seven sailors adrift, leaving them no clothes, food, or anything to drink. The mutinous crew sailed Hudson's ship *Discovery* back to England where, when all the investigations were over, the mutineers shockingly went free.

Whatever happened to Hudson and his men? No one will ever know. Their ghosts must remain for those who still come to these shores and try to imagine who came before them. There were stories, of course. Some of those who came later claimed to have seen blue-eyed men dressed like savages. Even a Hudson's Bay Company man said he had talked to a Cree Indian with "surprisingly pale skin" who claimed to have descended from Englishmen. Maybe Henry Hudson's genes have been left along shores of the sea that bears his name; his daring reputation is surely there.

Such a body of water is due its reverence. Freezing and melting through the circle of the year, it carries not only our bears, but the bears' seals, and whales, walrus, arctic char. To go beyond the land's edge, one must change his mode of motion in a profound way; he must undergo a metamorphosis—one that likely did not take place for a couple of million years until, by intent or by accident, those first early men ventured away from the solid ground that held and nurtured them. We would stay here, looking about us, trying to know just a little of this cold neighborhood.

The migration routes of polar bears in general, and these bears in particular, have for the most part been unknown or misunderstood, depending upon the logical rigor of the speaker. For a long time bears were thought to wander the Arctic with no faithfulness to any territory. And stories of bears on ice floes way down in the Atlantic or Pacific were likely true, but these sightings now seem to have been exceptions. Only after transmitters were placed on the bears did some of their pattern emerge (it is still emerging). While the bears were at the Cape during the fall, their behavior was observed from a tower like the ones seen in large forests elsewhere—put up to watch for forest fires. Here, of course, there was no forest to burn. But observers were put in the tower for days on end, blizzards or no, to gather information. They couldn't come down because of the bears.

Tomorrow we would go to the tower, because earlier in the week Len had left a small track vehicle there for use as a back-up if something went wrong and also for those who wished to use it to reconnoiter. On its top he had strapped a skidoo for another back-up. Out here we were beyond any immediate help and, oddly, all Len had brought was a borrowed CB radio that was never to work to our good.

As it was, the bunkhouse towed behind was the only artifice I could see. Such a situation is, even today, not difficult to experience. Anyone with a tent or a canoe can still (thankfully) go to a place in a forest where what he brings is the only collection of artifice, and he, the only animal that knows he is one. Here, however, the starkness of the Cape multiplied the effect of isolation.

Dark was falling rapidly and everyone scurried to make us safe before we could not (should not) go out. The bunkhouse was pulled by a long stiff bridle of pipe, then attached to a steel cable. This had to be unhooked before the Buggy could be backed up, carefully, to the little bunkhouse door. The back end of the Buggy had a steel platform where one could stand, and where a steel ladder was let down once the vehicle had stopped. To link the Buggy with the bunkhouse, the ladder had to be dumped on the ground. Since the Buggy has no brakes and weighs several tons it is hard to get just the right distance. Because of the nature of one of the doors, the steel platform had to be four or five inches away from the threshold of the bunkhouse. This short distance would become during our sojourn sometimes a gulf, a line of demarcation, and sometimes a source of jeopardy. We linked up on a piece of rocky ground that was not level, but because dark had fallen Len said it would be better to wait until tomorrow to move.

For the bunkhouse to become in fact a bunkhouse, it had to disgorge all the boxes of hamburger and stew meat and chicken, which were now placed on top of the bunkhouse where it was well below freezing. Then boxes of bread, which would freeze rapidly too, had to be removed. Throughout the disgorging, one person at least had to watch out for bears. All too often in bear country someone has gotten too busy fixing his flat tire or working his trapline, only to find his heart suddenly beating double, his adrenaline at flood tide.

4

"OK, you guys."

The day according to Guravich had begun. He came from the forward vehicle that was backed up to our tiny bunkhouse, stepped across the narrow metal platform, briefly cracked the door to make his reveille, then ducked back to where he belonged. Six of us made no move in our sleeping bags. It was dark and it would be dark for another hour and a half. No one wanted to make the move from his chrysalis; no one thought he would fly. It was too cold to fly.

Four bunks occupied each side of the bunkhouse, and some of us were on the up side. Because the Buggy was tilted ten degrees from the tundra below, all of us spent that night feeling as if we might roll out into the aisle. If you had a top bunk, the anxiety was heightened. Even asleep your body kept part of itself taut to keep from rolling. My neck and side were slightly sore.

The bunkhouse was nothing but a plywood shell around a skeleton of two-by-fours. There was one small sliding window on each wall. Even if a polar bear stood on his hind legs his head and front paws could not reach the windows. So I was told.

During the night, as the wind hurled against the tiny box here on the Canadian tundra, I had some doubts about its sturdiness.

About two or three in the morning, the rocking seemed worse than before and strangely regular. Len struggled out of his warm sleeping bag and yelled outside. The regular rocking stopped. Bears. A couple of adult bears were having their early morning workout. They were standing upright and shoving our little matchbox of security. Later I would see them rear up and come crashing down on thick ice, breaking it as they searched for something to eat. I thought about our thin plywood as I drifted in and out of sleep.

Len was the first to get out after Guravich's reveille. He reached for the propane lantern and turned it halfway up. Not since the early fifties had I been penned up with a group of men whom I had not chosen and whom, should things go wrong, I could not leave. In the army in the fifties, I found many guys I could have done without: thugs that were out of work, kids running away from home, and some actually trying to get to Korea. Here, of course, I had chosen to come, specifically here, which may seem a special species of madness: it was thirty below; I was lying in my sleeping bag on a board, and was surrounded outside the bunkhouse by North America's most ferocious carnivore.

After Len, one of the two Mounties, Eric Luke, dropped down from his upper bunk and began piling on his layers of clothing. Especially important were the boots with thick felt liners and thin wire screens between these and the bottoms of the boots so that the moisture would gather and freeze there. Chaos resulted if more than two or three of us tried to get dressed in the aisle. At this point in the "getting up," all but one of the bunks was occupied. And in the beginning, boxes of canned goods and fresh vegetables and liquor were stowed anywhere there was not clothing or gear.

Much though one might want to stay in his bunk, harassment from the forward vehicle soon got us moving. Because three men slept on boards over the seats, independent movement was mostly out of the question. Before breakfast could be started, the boards had to be handed from man to man and lashed to the top of the bunkhouse so that all the bedding could be placed on the top bunks.

Guravich had been up at least half an hour before anyone else. As we were to discover, he went to bed around eight-thirty. There were only two others in the group who could go to sleep that early. At least Guravich had coffee going by the time all of us got forward; that seemed the only consolation for this ridiculous reveille.

The Buggy was much colder than the bunkhouse, for several reasons. Both sides were lined with windows that could slide down like those on school buses, and the floor was metal plate. During the day the pot-bellied stove was kept going. That plus all the human bodies made it bearable. At night the stove was inevitably allowed to go out. Once even a bottle of cooking wine froze solid.

Abruptly the doors were opened by someone from the Buggy. Harry and I had gotten up none too soon. The wind swept across the platform, threatening to rip the doors off their hinges. First the foam mattresses were piled on two of the top bunks, then the plywood bed boards were put on top of the bunkhouse. If they were kept horizontal, the man who was atop the metal ladder that was coated with ice was a prime candidate for becoming a sailplane—one that would land him among some hungry bears. And a fall here would not receive immediate medical attention.

Now that the pressure was off from up forward, and breakfast-making proceeded, we were able to take a more leisurely pace, stowing our sleeping bags and having a go at the brushing of teeth. Filling a plastic glass with water from a jerry can, one brushed near the door and rinsed through a crack. On the platform the wind was blowing at thirty-five miles an hour, and clean teeth didn't seem worth a wind tunnel test in the gray-dark of morning. Leaning over the crack to rinse my mouth, I suddenly looked into the dark, inquisitive eyes of a huge male bear. My first bear encounter was an intimate one! No doubt this was the fellow who'd been playing shake-the-wagon last night.

We all drifted forward. There was one bus seat to each member after the bed boards and mattresses were removed. All the seats were on the right; on the left was a long table where Guravich was putting together breakfast at one end.

I am not a heavy breakfast person. But when one is fed only at prescribed times of the day, as in the army, one eats. The smell of bacon alone can generate an appetite for me without much additional help. Fried eggs, rashers of bacon, browned scallops of potatoes. Our toaster was most novel. One simply pressed slices of bread on the sides of the iron wood stove and they stuck there, vertically, until they were done, whereupon they fell off.

Like some chief chef at the Four Seasons, Guravich took possession of the kitchen. Although unappointed and unelected, he clearly wanted to be cook. Later, when others offered to fix some favorite dish, their efforts were declined. Fussing over each pot, each pan, Guravich provided an amusing sideshow on this early morning. Several of us, including myself, had been instructed by long-distance phone to bring what are commercially known as "Handi-wipes." Five or six thousand ultimately arrived. Throughout the day we were urged, admonished even, to avail ourselves of these moistened, perfumed hand towels—before we ate, after we ate, and between meals for good measure.

Our daily regimen would require positioning the vehicle so that we'd have "clean" snow or otherwise interesting backgrounds on at least two sides, but especially facing the morning sun, then perhaps moving or shifting our position as the light shifted. This morning, though, the first morning, Len wanted to get the track vehicle, to have it close at hand. When he started the engine the bear that was hanging about went racing off, staying gone just long enough for Roy and Len to jump down, pick up the metal stairs, and fit them on in the up position. We could see several bears a mile away. As the Buggy lumbered and pitched over the rough ground, all the cooking gear, jars, what have you, slid about, just as though we were at sea.

I had been assured by some member of our party that the bears couldn't climb well. I wish I could now remember who that was. I knew black bears were good climbers, but of course they lived where there were trees. What greeted us at the track vehicle laid to rest that silly notion, but it had its comic side, too. The roof of the vehicle was perhaps six feet from the ground, and on top was the skidoo. Scattered all over the landscape were pieces of foam rubber. Bears had not only climbed on top, they had torn the skidoo seat to smithereens. It was evident from all the tracks that some kind of football game had taken place, the bears rollicking with their strange new toy. All this was funny to everyone but Len, who owned the skidoo. Fortunately they had not found a way into the vehicle itself.

Most of us chased about in the wind gathering up the debris while Len went to warm up the vehicle. The engine started up fine. When it was warm, he put it in gear and the universal joint promptly broke. That's when Len remembered he should have drained the old fluid, which had water in it, and added new. With the rear-end frozen, the shaft had merely snapped. Len had to verify this in the snow. On his back!

Although not unduly alarmed, he knew it was the better part of wisdom to have the back-up available. After Len and Roy conferred briefly, it was decided that Roy would take the skidoo back to Churchill, a much faster trip by skidoo than by Tundra Buggy. He would get the necessary parts and return the next morning. With the seat torn up, Roy would have a rough ride. Some of the larger pieces of foam were taped to the machine, and the high-powered rifle in the Buggy was given to him. He would be going all the way back through solid bear country, on an open skidoo. To make matters even dicier, Roy did not have that much experience on a skidoo—certainly not with this skidoo. He was a biologist more than a mechanic. Starting out, he killed the machine within fifty feet. We walked over with Len, who explained some of the eccentricities. Roy took off again. About a mile away, he got stuck or the machine stopped, we couldn't tell which. Off he went again. And truly, it happened a third time within our sight. I was very glad it was he going instead of me, but I must say my thoughts stayed with him. As far as hope without vision can go.

We climbed back up in the Buggy and motored over to the tower. Bruemmer, who had spent long days observing the bears the year before, talked of difficulties, of narrow escapes. He told about climbing all the way down the narrow steel ladder to the wooden platform on the first level—to answer nature's call. While he was there one day, an enterprising bear started up the ladder, and he had to slam the lid over the hole that permitted the ladder through. It was clearly Bruemmer that I should have asked about "climbing" bears.

As we chatted, a figure came loping down the esker toward us, a figure that, along with his kind, would almost steal the show from the bears. Moving toward us, then away, then back again was . . . an arctic fox. The essence of nimbleness, this great ball of fluff bore little relation to the creature crippling away from Joe's trap on three legs. Another one darted from an overturned oil drum, then dashed away, not in terror but not wanting to become pals, either. We investigated the drum and ascertained that it was their residence. A lemming's bones were near the opening.

Near the base of the tower was a large, strongly built steel cage. Researchers had entered the cage for various reasons and observed the bears from ground level and close by. No doubt the first man to test it was a brave soul. This was the same cage that has since been seen on the National Geographic special. I am a member of that society, read the magazine avidly, and try never to miss their television shows. But the show on the bears and the town of Churchill was not, in my opinion, one of their best. Now any reporter, any writer, has had others tell him that if they had been doing the piece, they wouldn't have done it that way. But I have asked a number of people what they remembered from this film—what stuck? And the answer is always chiefly two images, or one really extended image. The RCMP comes roaring up to the house of an Indian woman who has called in about a wandering bear. The camera locks onto this screaming, hysterical (or mock-hysterical) woman, afraid of being eaten by a bear. Without a commensurate image load to convey the more generally held attitude toward the bears, a single image like this becomes worse than none at all, if the film is to be about the town's relationship with the bears. As we know, equal footage is not necessarily equal impact.

Then there was the image of this cage. From inside the cage the camera records the bear's mouth gnawing on the bars. There was some other footage of bears, of course, but the filmic residue was the ferocity of the bears and the terror of the woman. Which is not what the film should have conveyed. The reality is not that.

With a failing economy, due in part to declining grain exports, the people of Churchill know their economy depends a great deal on people coming to see the bears in winter and the birds in summer. Further, they have so patently gotten along with this huge carnivore. The one man killed the next year was an Indian picking around in the recently burned-out ruin of a café—at night! People know, have been educated, not to walk about alone at night.

We scrambled back into the Buggy, sans Roy, intending to go to the end of the Cape and position ourselves for some good pictures of the foxes. As Len made the circle over the oval top esker, he heard a low grinding sound. The rest of us didn't know the vehicle well enough to sort out the sounds. But like a conductor hearing a distant, erring second violin in the storm of a symphony, Len cocked his head in concern, stopped, and leaped down to the ground. The lugs on the giant wheels had snapped.

The only reason the wheel didn't roll off, as it would have on an automobile, was that the hubs were very wide. Now, however, everyone began to realize our predicament. We were separated some distance from the bunkhouse, which held most of the supplies. There would be no sleeping, at least not in a prone position. There were nine of us left. Even if we had had a large enough jack, Len had no spare lugs. And Roy was gone in the skidoo, the only way back to town.

If we stayed, at least we would be resting on four wheels. Len decided to gamble, and we made an attempt to reach the bunkhouse. We could live quite snugly there, taking pictures. Len asked Eric to walk alongside the Buggy, to warn him if the wheel started to work its way off.

"Better take your heater, Eric," advised Jerry, reaching back for the old cop lingo of Dick Tracy and Sam Spade. Both Mounties had brought their sidearms. Jerry kept his close by. Several bears were visible about a quarter-mile away, but they were not yet moving in our direction.

As long as we could keep the Buggy tilted slightly to the right, on the right side of the esker, all was fine. But that wasn't always possible, and there was much gnashing of teeth before we made it back to the bunkhouse. You would have thought we'd finally made it back home from overseas, instead of reaching a mere twelve-by-eight plywood box slumped on a cold tundra esker. But that was our home for now. It meant warmth, food, even liquor.

Although there was no choice about where we put the Buggy (we were grateful to be where we were), it turned out to be admirably positioned for sunrise and sunset. But we also looked out over the big flat white expanse of a frozen lake that was just on the other side of an old beach ridge and was not affected by the tides. On the other side of the esker we had just traveled was the jagged, icy terrain where the tides cracked the ice to beauty.

Our concern over the mechanical trouble had evaporated, and because the bunkhouse had been still, the bears had gotten used to it. They would be drawn to us out of curiosity if nothing else. Particularly with the smells from our lunch wafting out the one cracked window.

To entice the bears toward places we could not move to, we broke open two cans of sardines and heated them on the Coleman. Then someone jumped down the ladder in front and raced out to put the sardines where they would attract the bears. The oil was left in the can on the burner to send more scent out the window. This distance would be no test of a bear's nose. It has been reported that a bear that was nineteen miles downwind of a dead whale made a beeline for it. Unfortunately today's wind was from the northwest and blew the scent out to sea. It was not to matter.

The question of baiting the bears turned out to be a matter of tension between Roy and Dan, though most of us were oblivious to it during our stay. There had been some conflict between them a year or two before, when Roy was with the Department of Natural Resources. I am not sure what it had to do with. But Roy didn't approve of using bait beyond the Buggy to lure the bears into "good" photographic position.

Putting out food for animals often engages the issue of altering their behavior. It is very likely true that if an animal associates a certain place or object with food—all things being equal—he is going to come there. If you plant cereal grains in Iowa or Nebraska, for example, the geese are going to stop there; and many of the geese and ducks that used to come from Canada to Louisiana quit coming—the well-known "short-stopping" problem. People who feed wild birds at their homes run the same risk. That is why northern bird lovers are urged not to continue feeding birds that should be flying south. Maybe it is the "degree" of contact that is at issue. But in a way the question reminds me of

Heisenberg's Uncertainty Principle. He was talking about measuring the position and velocity of subatomic particles, but he noted that by measuring one state the other was altered, or made uncertain. At least that is how I understand him. It's similar to measuring the pressure in a tire; when you apply the gauge, you alter the amount of air that was in the tire. Now if this seems a long way from altering bear behavior, let me try to bring matters back. The moment the human consciousness enters any picture, matters have probably been altered to some degree. But surely the moment the animal sees you in any circumstance, he has been changed. Even if we were to walk naked upon the land, revealing what little hair we have left, signaling some commonality with other mammals, our bringing the planning brain with us alters our relationship to these creatures. The effect is greatly magnified if one comes in a machine. And if the machine has the smell of bacon coming out the window, it is perhaps a "quantum leap." Perhaps this reflection has become too Jesuitical, yet whether to alter or not to alter behavior is not so simple as some seek to make it.

Ethical questions aside (man's "right" to do, etc.), turning the bears into a trained act would be like Jack killing the goose that laid the golden egg. In a very limited sense, once the "natural" behavior is changed the animal loses a lot of its fascination for those interested in wild nature. So, we're back to Churchill *needing* the people who want to see the bears.

In a much broader sense, the loss of "naturally" behaving bears or birds may keep us from learning what they have to teach us: one more living species that so far has made it, and made it in its unique way. In this particular instance, it just happens to be an alpha predator, who had mostly man, the superalpha, to look out for. But the bear is no more important than the ringed seal he kills to live, nor the fish the seal kills to live. After all, it is just our narcissism that prefers living things that look like us, or a bit like us.

One might profitably examine why it is that he or she is more fascinated with carnivores or with predators who are at the "top" of the pyramid: birds of prey, lions, tigers, bears. Not necessarily because this preference may reflect some hidden guilt of blood, but because such an examination might pressure us to look hard at our "noble" feelings about caring for animals. If what is really taking place is some sort of transference, then there is a kind of self-centeredness involved that at least needs to be acknowledged, rather than passed off as a reverence for life. It may be that one's desire to "protect" a lion or a bear borders on the inexplicable. It may also be true that merely being unable to explain or completely define something does not mean that it doesn't exist. Yet in matters of the limits of appropriate behavior, one is so often asked for evidence—even the kind of evidence one is required to give in a court of law.

This question of caring for, or "loving," a bear over a bat, reminds me of Miller Williams' poem "Euglena."[1]

Euglena

Microscopic monster
germ father, founder of the middle way
who first saw fit to join no clan
but claim the best of both
you are more than clever.

Swimming, you go to what meal is.
Green, you make what isn't.

Fencerider
mimicked by more than have heard of
Jesus or Nietzsche

you've held your own for twenty
million years

who might have been a tulip
or a tiger

you shrewd little bastard

I suspect that the main statement of the poem is not to ridicule the primitive organism known as euglena; it has to do more with fence-riding. In the manner of good poems, it leaves you not with some jingle or saw that avoids the complexity and paradox we confront in our existence. The poet may really prefer a tulip or tiger, or at least these species of beauty, but I doubt that he thinks the euglena's adaptive response to the world is inferior to the tulip's or the tiger's. He may. But the euglena certainly has a no-less-amazing strategy for survival and has shown itself to be successful at maintaining its kind. Yet, in the world's wildlife court, not many are holding any brief for the euglena. That may be because it is not known to be threatened, but somehow I doubt it. And who trembles before muscling some bacterium around?

Our sardines were in place and the wind was picking up, but it was not yet blowing snow. Soon a small bear moved down the esker following the scent. The windows of the Buggy started dropping as the picture-taking began. With all the windows down, the inside became quite cold. But working the camera quickly made gloves nearly impossible. Almost no one had the same kind of equipment, except Guravich and me. We both had Minoltas. Bruemmer had an older Nikon. Several of us had powered film advancers, but Bruemmer just kept clicking away with his quieter manual advance. Sometimes I think he became annoyed with the persistent whirring sound of the automatic advancers. I expect he quite deliberately avoided overly complicated apparatus because he was so often in remote places in the north where there was no way to get anything fixed. He even had some of his cameras degreased so that the moving parts would not jam because of the cold.

Suddenly, from the southwest, I could see them coming: two really big males pacing toward us. The speed with which they moved was deceptive. In what seemed just a few seconds they had made it from a mile away. Their huge paws left tracks in the snow that were a foot in diameter. As they drew up to the Buggy, the massiveness of their forelegs (one wants to call them arms after watching the bears for very long) is awesome. Bruemmer comments that he has seen a bear smash and drag an eight-hundred-pound bearded seal out of the ice with one paw. And here we were tantalizing them with sardines.

These males weighed about a thousand pounds apiece. For short distances they could run at a speed of thirty-five miles per hour. The head and body length of polar bears ranges up to eight feet and up to better than four feet in height. As far as length and height, there isn't much difference between brown bears (*Ursus arctos*) and polar bears (*Ursus maritimus*); Kodiaks are a little heavier. Yet the polar bear is sometimes described as the largest predator on earth. That's because of the way these bears make their living. Grizzlies are not primarily predators; they eat berries, grubs, and fish. But the polar bear has adapted to his icy world by being essentially a killer of seals and sometimes whales.

Both brown and white bears evolved from a common ancestor, the extinct cave bear (*Ursus etruscus*) who lived during the Pleistocene. Polar bears and brown bears are obviously close relatives, for in captivity they will breed together. Yet there are several differences besides their color. The brown bear is more "dish faced," while the polar bear has a longer skull, and his nose has been described as "Roman." His neck is longer, too. Very significantly, the relatively smaller molars and the longer canine teeth of the polar bear reflect his carnivorous way of life.

Having eaten the sardines out from the Buggy and not getting any more, these two big males reared up on the side of the Buggy. Large though their heads appear at this distance, they seem gracile.

Eric and Treul went out on the back platform, braving the cold to get a better angle. Such ventures in the frigid wind served as a reminder of the excellent insulation the bears carried with them. When bears have been eating well, they can have up to four inches of fat on parts of their bodies. In addition, their hairs have been found to be hollow. Visible light is reflected, but the ultra-violet light is transmitted down the hair to the black skin. It is difficult, though, not to anthropomorphize a bear, not to feel that he is freezing to death. After all, he can even stand erect like us, at least for brief periods.

As the light began to fail, the wind was clearly becoming stronger. Several other bears were appearing, beyond our camera range, looking ghostly in the dark. Lenses were unscrewed and packed away and all of us who lived in the bunkhouse took our camera bags back with us. Very much like folks who had finished any average day's work, we now closed up the shop. This would be our pattern every day. Seven of us leaving, crossing the platform and the five or six inches between the two vehicles which became a chasm, a small gorge, a valley whose passage meant a stepping-over into another state.

In the beginning Guravich, Treul, and Bruemmer all remained behind in the Buggy—Guravich to cook the evening meal, Treul and Bruemmer tidying up their areas, and Bruemmer making notes in his field diary. The other seven of us gathered in the bunkhouse. Ultimately, the centrifugal force of the gathering in the rear would draw at least two of those initially left behind.

Len had brought along his radio, which also had a tape player with it. But first the Canadian Broadcasting Company had a news program that he tuned for after our day's shooting. And there was a weather report. The radio and all the liquor were stashed on the single vacant top bunk. It became the bar. This was where the Caesars were introduced to the tyros. A Caesar is essentially a Bloody Mary, but one made with clamato juice (tomato juice and clam juice), substantial doses of Tabasco sauce, Worchester-shire, and even a sprig of celery.

The weather report this evening was grim. A real blizzard was heading our way, the overture to which we were already feeling. Roy's return seemed unlikely, that is, if Roy had made it out in the first place. During the evening Len tried to reach Churchill on the CB, but without success.

"Everybody got one of these things during the rage, but now nobody listens anymore. Of course, I don't even know if I'm getting out." The CB was forward, where the driver of the Buggy sat. During supper later that night, the only voice we could hear was a truck driver booming all the way up from Alabama. Even though he was probably overpowered, we must have been getting a "skipped" signal. Len tried to contact him, but got no response. It's bad enough to break down on a highway in, say, West Texas at night, but at least you're on a road there.

Following supper, and after the dishes had been washed, high talk was carried on in the bunkhouse. Very shortly after everything was clean, Guravich began asking for the bed boards that were lashed to the top. The ladder was brought out and Len undertook the precarious operation. We worried about the icy ladder. Some of the bears were all the way under the Buggy where they couldn't be seen. Some were covered up in a nearby snowbank. But no one would be able to get back in quickly enough, because the steel steps couldn't be put up. The only way to reach safety was by running all the way to the front and trying to scramble up the front tire and into the driver's seat. But luck was with us and Len safely executed the transfer. After the bed boards were sent forward, the mattresses were passed along, and then the guys could sit on their bunks.

These gatherings each evening were very special for me, and I think for the others, too. The day's shooting was over, and the windows in the Buggy were closed against the cold. We'd collect our camera gear and parkas and step across that little windy space of the rear deck, across the few inches of abyss wherein the bear might be and into our small enchanted space. One light had failed, the direct light of the sun, but another light was lit.

At least a few times in one's life, if he is lucky, he will have moments when all spirits seem to flow benignly. As one ascends the ladder of numbers, often the possibilities decrease. Most often spirits seem able to gather in twos. A man with his wife or girlfriend, or with a best buddy. Thereon the difficulties multiply as in calculus: two body motion problems are one thing; three body problems much more complicated, and so on. Having experienced at least one other "transcendent" time in my life, I recognized when I was in the presence of it again.

Partly I think it was that each member of our group had earned his way in some field. He was interested in what he was doing, and had achieved some measure of recognition in it. Since our fields were mostly disparate, there was that jealous-free possibility, that opening out, that mutual respect that can come from one accomplished journeyman to another. I have thought several times that a master carpenter, a master boat-builder, might have a kind of common understanding about the deep things of the world that could be shared, perhaps nonverbally, with a master violinist or a master physicist—that Einstein and Bach would have understood much the same thing. Insofar as there is one thing to understand.

Slowly the story of Bob Delareuelle's life unfolded a little. Bob had retired as a Pan-Am pilot and was living it up in California. He had gotten hooked up with a marine reserve squadron in 1932 while he was getting his degree at Berkeley. By 1938 he was a naval aviator, and from 1939 to 1972 he was a Pan-Am pilot. But that didn't end his military flying. During World War II he flew for the army, wore an army uniform, flew army planes, and still worked for Pan-Am—flying cargo from Miami to Rio, then across Africa to Chabua, India, the beginning of the Hump. Those were the illustrious years when we still thought Chiang Kai-shek and Madame Chiang were heroes fighting for Methodists and democracy, only later to discover they were chiefly gangsters. Bob knew "Pappy" Boyington of Flying Tigers' fame. Boyington finally quit flying his P-40 in disgust over the corruption of the Chiang government.

Before he retired at the mandatory sixty years of age, Bob had flown 400 flights into Saigon, Cam Ranh Bay, Da Nang in Vietnam. All told, his log book showed 25,704 hours and 7,500,000 miles! Now he does gigs like following polar bears around, or going on pack trips down in Lower California. Bob had some kind of a camera, but you could tell that wasn't the big stick for him. He liked the comradery and just took the thing between his big fists to go along. He kept the best records of what bears he saw, how many birds and what kind, and turned the information over to the Canadian Wildlife Service people on his way out.

The two Mounties were a slightly different cup of tea. Cops in general, it seems to me, end up being more distant, chiefly because it's part of their trade. And if they've been around very long, they've even learned to be that way with some of their own. As "The Shadow" knew and explained to us over the radio in the forties, "Evil lurks in the hearts of men." Jerry Anderson had originally been head of the Churchill RCMP detachment and had rotated to Winnipeg. Apparently, everybody has to do a hard-time post and Churchill was considered to be one, though certainly not the hardest. There were dillies all over the Northwest Territories. Before it was time for him to go he told his old buddy Eric some of the good points, and Eric came to the detachment next. Eric had been doing lie detector work before he took over. Jerry was now head of Intelligence back in Winnipeg. He had taken a lot of wildlife pictures during his tour and had placed a number of them in magazines. Now he was back with Eric, partly for the pictures but partly out of nostalgia for Churchill.

Mounties refer to the other guys in the RCMP as "Members." From my little experience the "Members" seem a tighter group than the FBI, and certainly more so than any state police. Maybe I'm reading the others wrong, but the Mounties have such a long tradition behind them, and the image that has captured the world's imagination has not been severely tarnished by exposés. They still use the famous red uniforms for parades or special events. They still do the "Musical Ride" on their horses. The training they go through initially is much more like boot camp in the army or marines than the usual police training.

There were six or eight men in the Churchill detachment. I have subsequently been in smaller communities in the Arctic where there may be only one or two Mounties for a gigantic chunk of land. Carrying oneself with bearing is a necessity in order to maintain any order. Otherwise something amorphous like "the law," something written down in Ottawa, doesn't have a lot of meaning in a remote Eskimo community. This bearing, or stance, contributes to the apparent distance between cops and other folks. But at least for moments, as the nights and days passed, Eric and Jerry also reflected the magic of the circle.

As the evenings went on I saw the gathering as a circle having a vortex, a flow of experiences and emotions and events around an axis. The bears were that axis. This gathering was like a star creation—the motion that begins to collect hydrogen atoms across the vastnesses of space on the way to their own gathering which is unknown and unrealized, but implicit. From Fred Treul casting brass in Milwaukee and dreaming of birds, to Harry Albers dissecting a dog's muscles or cutting off frozen pelican feet, to Mounted Policemen who looked for a respite from the carnivory of man—from all these atoms of men would come the consort, the comitatus.

Such a time is mostly a lucky vortex of mysterious lines, and the lines are infinite. As far as human time goes, existence is not in a curve. These lines won't cross again. They are as transient as the light on the tops of waves that never repeat themselves in Keats's "Ode to Melancholy." Keats urges that when melancholy descends "Then glut thy sorrow on a morning rose,/ Or on the rainbow of the salt sand-wave," for "Beauty must die/ And Joy, is ever at his lips/ Bidding adieu." The one who knows melancholy's shrine is the one "whose strenuous tongue/ Can burst Joy's grape against his palate fine."

Insurance executive and poet Wallace Stevens leads us in a similar way to grasp such transient moments of fellowship, which are enormously heightened with the recognition that we will die.[2]

> Supple and turbulent, a ring of men
> Shall chant in orgy on a summer morn
> Their boisterous devotion to the sun,
> Not as a god, but as a god might be,
> Naked among them, like a savage source.
> Their chant shall be a chant of paradise
> Out of their blood, returning to the sky;
>
> ....
>
> That choir among themselves long afterward
> They shall know well the heavenly fellowship
> Of men that perish and of summer morn.
>
> ("Sunday Morning")

And this fellowship of men that perish could celebrate itself of a winter's night, too.

Although I did not interrogate the group, I doubt there was anyone there who thought he would be personally immortal. Those who had not been in combat of some kind were otherwise close to matters of death, whether as policeman or veterinarian, or as former civilian prisoner of war. Confronted with the details of carnivory—which is always clearer outside the city where the facts are hidden, as are the events of birth and death—the starkness of this "old chaos of the sun" is more often unlit than lit during winter. All of this only served to make the lines of descent to the grave clearer and clarified the beauty of the experience, to elevate the bear, the circle of men, the circle of bear and men, to the plane of "the rainbow of the salt sand-wave."

I am not sure whether the specialness of the convergence was felt by everyone then, or whether all felt it only later, though some say yes, because later and when it could be held up to subsequent experiences, it shone in comparison. Decompressing in

Winnipeg, and then at our various destinations, we all felt an immensely poignant and clear sense of loss.

As any of our evenings wore on, nature would call, and the proper place for relief was off the side of the platform. One had to be sure to gauge the wind right, of course. Firewood was stacked high on one side. If the wind was not altogether against you, it was most convenient to use the other side. But over there was a five-gallon bucket that contained fermenting whale skin with some fat attached, which we called by the Eskimo word *muktuk* (sometimes spelled *maktark* or *maktar*). We had gotten it from a driver of a dog team in Churchill who fed beluga whale to his dogs. For a bear it is the *pièce de résistance*. Ripe as it was, it could draw a bear for miles. In its semirotten condition, it was exceedingly pungent, even while frozen. One always had to be careful not to get any on his gloves or clothing, because it was with you for the trip.

On such an excursion to the platform, one of the fellows gave out a yell. Standing on tiptoes, a bear had reached his paw up above the floor, trying to get at the *muktuk*. Such circumstances greatly heightened the adventure of taking a piss in the night. Stored right there next to our door, this substance seemed by itself to dub our bunkhouse-home-saloon-music hall. From this night on it was the "Muktuk Saloon," the "Muktuk" for short.

5

Our buffeting this second night was not by bears, but by the whistling, howling wind. Because the propane heater had to be left on, we were concerned about getting enough oxygen in the room. The first night had left some of us with a slight headache. Thereafter we tried to crack by an inch one of the small sliding windows. Tonight's wind was so terrific that snow had piled up at the foot of Eric's upper bunk and ice had gathered in the aluminum track. This was a major storm. Roy would not be able to get back from Churchill. So we would be stationary, but at least we had all we needed.

The next morning Guravich decided we all needed a dose of Red River Cereal, many of us for the first time. This apparently functioned for him like Proust's *petite madeleine,* setting off all sorts of memories of his growing up in Winnipeg. The cereal is named after the Red River of the North, one of two significant rivers that flow through Winnipeg, the other being the Assiniboine.

Guravich's parents had emigrated from Lithuania during the first part of the present century. Even though he has lived and worked since the early fifties in the United States, Guravich still holds his Canadian citizenship. He had taken a doctorate in agricultural genetics from the University of Wisconsin and found work in Greenville, Mississippi, at the cotton research station there. But it wasn't long before he was taking pictures, and soon he was making a living taking pictures.

His lips smacked as he stirred what looked like two gallons of Red River Cereal, no doubt thinking of frosty mornings in his Winnipegian childhood. He claimed it was good for the digestion (it probably was), and he was much concerned with such matters. In motels he would often order some sort of bran flakes, and just as frequently he'd say "flabber-gassy" after a cartoon figure's description of the cereal *he* ate in the cartoon. His concerns with digestion seemed as intense as his concern for cleanliness, his insistence on the use of those Handi-wipes that made our grungy bunch smell very flowery.

The makeshift toilet was—fortunately and unfortunately—inside the Buggy. Fortunate in that it would have been impossible at these temperatures to endure the session outdoors—unfortunate in that there was no escape for the others. Use of the toilet unfailingly provided a stream of scatological jokes and abuse, with the expectant breakfasters demanding that the performer use the box of matches left in the enclosure. Sometimes the joking took on the taxonomy of ethnic descent—Lithuanian, Latvian, Hungarian, and Ukrainian being only a few of the choices.

This morning's maiden performance for Red River Cereal was ruined because the cook doubled or tripled the amount of salt that was necessary (if any was—here the remembrance of cereal past, its preparation, went a little cloudy). There was a lot of stirring of bowls and looking away, until someone who declined to insist the emperor had on clothes declared, "Man, is this ever salty"—which brave remark was straightaway confirmed by the more reticent. Toast and jam replaced our bowls, and that morning the bears of Churchill were introduced to a salty version of what otherwise was probably good cereal.

Suddenly Bruemmer, usually quiet, not given to rugby-style humor, exclaimed, "Look, there's our fox." And sure enough, whether one of those from the tower or a brother of theirs, here he came in all his delicate white, loping down the esker—just like it was nothing to be out for a walk at 10° below zero in wind that seemed as though it should knock him off his feet.

The arctic fox looks heavier than it is. The red fox is bigger, but he would look even larger by comparison if both he and the tiny arctic fox (5 kg) shed all their fur. The arctic fox's hair is 50 mm long as compared to the slightly less 45–46 mm of the red fox, but the red fox weighs twice as much. The arctic fox may have to sustain −94°F, of course, like the polar bear; but the relative size is highly significant, the advantage going to the bear. In addition, the arctic fox must live in the most variable external temperatures on earth. For comparison, consider that a naked man starts reacting to 50°F of cold. That is, his metabolic thermostat cuts on and has to start producing heat. The arctic fox's thermostat doesn't kick in until −40°F.

"Give me a sardine, give me a sardine," Bruemmer said. I wrestled with a can opener while he lowered a front window. Quickly he flung a sardine as far as he could. And we waited. The fox loped along like yesterday, thirty or forty yards toward us, then away. But something in the wind finally turned him toward us seriously. More sardines out the windows. Thus the Great Sardine Throw of Cape Churchill continued. By the middle of the morning, the fox would dart within twenty feet of the Buggy, grab a piece of sardine, and take off down the esker.

All this soon drew the biggest meat eater of all over. We had two bears that Bruemmer guessed weighed eight or nine hundred pounds each, standing out from our windows wanting their sardines, too. The light was not the best and the wind kept snow particles in the air, swirling and eddying, but we clicked away. At least it could be said that such weather was truly what the bears usually lived, killed, and ate in.

When a bear kills a big seal, he may well leave a lot of the meat, taking mostly the blubber, assuming he has not gone too long without other food. That is why the arctic fox follows him onto the ice, hoping to find what the bear doesn't need or want. This time of year, though, the bears haven't had much to eat either. After lunch, a big bone was thrown fifty or sixty feet out in the snow to get the bears off at a good distance, but the fox raced in and grabbed the bone, which was half as big as he was. We laughed at the little fox trying to get the big bone down the esker before the bears could reach it. For now at least, he kept going with his precious bonanza and disappeared in the driving snow.

Around ten o'clock the next morning, although there was still wind, the air had cleared. We were all surprised to see a helicopter descend far away at the tower. The sighting generated a lot of hope, because we needed to make contact with the outside. In just a few minutes the chopper headed over our way, scaring the bears in the immediate area. The Canadian Wildlife folks, whom Len knew, were just dropping by because they were in the area, not having the foggiest notion that we were in any kind of trouble. Although Churchill is very small, neither of the two men on board had talked to Roy. So Len gave them the huge studs that held the hub onto the wheel, and asked them to tell Roy to fix them. An hour after they left it started snowing again. But at least we knew the message would get in that we were down.

We had become so much a fixture of the landscape that it was not long before bears from all directions came drifting back on the scene. The snow flurries ebbed and flowed and at times even seemed to warm a little. The bears seemed alert and curious to walk over to the other bears, who stood about singly or in pairs. And then it started.

The suddenness of the beginning of play-fighting requires a quick hand on the camera shutter, and often play-fighting doesn't take place right next to the vehicle. Often it is altogether beyond effective camera range for anything except a record shot. I was very lucky on this trip, as I witnessed two extended sessions within range *and* I wasn't at the end of a roll, which happens to the best. It's often too late to go to another camera body. Once it starts, the playing can go on for quite some time, or the spectacular part of it may end after a couple of minutes.

Although there may be a number of bears within the circumference of sight, up to thirty or forty on magic occasions, they are not all known to each other in the same way. It is common to see two or three bears standing around, or lying down, and a fourth bear from elsewhere approach them. He always circles the group and only comes in to them if there is some kind of sign; perhaps he recognizes a familiar smell.

Two old buddies, however, may meet, touch noses, and one of them may put a big paw on the other's shoulder. Suddenly both will rear up in a standing position, looking for all the world like two giant sumo wrestlers waiting for the right time to get the first advantage. One bear may end up flat on its back, still wrestling, or the other may wait politely until its partner gets back up. Watching this is like watching two giant white puppies play.

Most of the photographs in this book that depict two bears in combat are of this kind of mock-combat. Play-fighting sometimes continues throughout the morning and, after a nap, begins again in the afternoon. The exertion certainly costs the bears a lot of calories at a time when their food supply is exceedingly limited. One has to ask why an animal would do this? What would it contribute to his welfare, which is another way of saying, how will such behavior help to pass on his genes to the next generation? Apparently in the process of Darwinian natural selection, play-fighting serves some purpose. Interestingly, play seems to be limited to the higher vertebrates. That may be one reason why we in the Buggy, like humans everywhere, are fascinated with the play of animals: it reminds us of ourselves. Both our play and the play of others are pleasures. But what is the serious purpose for the bears? Any kind of definitive answer is not in yet. But I think it is first a way to practice, to stay in shape for the very serious business of fighting in earnest over mates in the spring. It may secondarily be a way of maintaining skills the bear needs to defend its own seal kill, if, that is, it doesn't want to share it.

Anyone who has watched dogs wrestle and tussle with each other (like young men, also) knows that these are the same moves he sees, only exaggerated, when dogs actually fight. Further, the bears, like dogs and men, can begin playing, and the play can either through intensity or accident become the real thing very rapidly. For bears and dogs, at least, such real fighting drops quickly back to play, or ceases, when it is not "over" something like food or females to start with. Play-fighting is one of the most exciting parts of bear behavior. And if one can get off rapid shots the photographs can be spectacular.

The reason for, the meaning of, photographing the bears and foxes varied among us. Those of us who were nonprofessionals (meaning here, those not intending to sell the images), depending on individual ardor, might merely be taking back a record of the trip. This could be a way of demonstrating to those back home that he did indeed see these things, a way of authenticating his journey. Too, the pictures might serve the function that a pair of antlers or a skin serves, that of a trigger for the memory, stimulating the recall of a significant event. Photography is a way for others who have not had such an experience to partly share it. Of course, the photograph is not "the experience." It is at best one aspect of an experience once removed. And in this respect, what is true of the nonprofessional's work is also true of the professional's.

The experience itself was one that took place in time, was in a state of flux. And the photograph begins the distortion of that experience by "freezing" a moment in time. A vicarious, "imaginative" participation shared by a friend was unlike seeing a bear or a fox while he moved, felt the cold, heard his sounds, and so on. And then there is the further distortion of presenting what is at least a three-dimensional reality in two dimensions. Of course

Tundra siesta

Ptarmigan cock in summer

Ptarmigan hen in summer

"Magnum"

Battle scars

Hostility

Heels over head

Laid back

"I would like the front seat"

A bear and a Buggy

Joe Kowal with his catch

Three in a day bed

Play-fighting: a sequence

A little fox amid big bear tracks

Snow vixen

Equipoise

Coexistence

"What's up?"

that is the method in painting, but one always concludes that painting is someone's "interpretation" of what happened or what appeared. With photographs we are sometimes inclined to think that this representation of what happened or what appeared is what was. After all, the very light particle-waves that were reflected from the bear struck the chemicals of the film—the very photons.

Yet we know that even though the bear and the light, in their coming together and parting, determine a great deal of what finally appears on the negative or the print, there is also a kind of interpretation or shaping by the photographer. He decides how much light to let into the film, what angle of light to use, and of course at what moment in time to stop the subject. All of this is a kind of interpretation, or certainly a selecting and shaping, part of the artifice. So when the pictures are finally developed and shown, what is shown is what *one* person thought was important and how he went about "bringing that version home." If he is like most, he will not present everything he initially selected. He will greatly pare down what he chooses to present—on the basis of technical execution and on the basis of the arrangement of the subjects. For example, because the foxes move so swiftly and agitatedly, there will often be many poor results. The head may be hidden; the face may be turned away.

Just as important, in all of this, is what the photographer did not photograph, much less crop from a picture. And here, one can test whether the photographer is giving the public "what it wants," or whether he has some other purpose: for example, demonstrating as many aspects of a cycle of the animal's life as possible, banal or ugly or not. His purpose might be to educate, or it might be to convey some moral vision. The photograph may serve as a powerful reminder to an increasingly urban people, cordoned off in cities and ghettoes of non-nature, that a human's life depends on devouring other life, that choosing to eat only plants (for reasons other than health) instead of members of the animal kingdom is either a subterfuge or avoidance. Since plants came first, create their own food without killing, and, like animals, contain protoplasm, grow, respond to the world, breed, and pass on their kind, one could argue that they have a special right to their own life in that they do not depend on devouring others in the kingdom of life. If one argues against animal food on the basis of animal pain, that argument can be confuted by painless death, should the matter come down to that.

It is true that all of this may not be found in any uncaptioned photograph, that a photograph cannot carry that kind of load. Susan Sontag has made the point very clearly. Photographs can't explain anything: one person looking at a bear killing a seal may well respond with disgust, and another viewer may respond with wonder. Sontag remarks, "In contrast to the amorous relation, which is based on how something looks, understanding is based on how it functions. And functioning takes place in time, and must be explained in time. Only that which narrates can make us understand."[3]

Photographers of animals generally present a "beautiful" animal, one that is not starving, one that has not been recently savaged by some other, one that has not contracted some disease. Now there is obviously a place for this. We wouldn't choose to strike down all the sculptures of ancient Greece because they do not represent an "average," or the common man. Nor would we argue that the "real" statement of a man's life is the sum of his ecstasy and his pain divided by two.

Yet what we are inclined to describe as "serious" in arts like poetry or fiction, drama or opera, manifests a range of experience, a complexity of emotions and values that is not evident in work done for entertainment. Admittedly, the purely visual arts present a problem here, for the images may have complexity of design, of balance (or unbalance), or color, and may be devoid of social comment. Some pictures, like Picasso's *Guernica* or Poussin's *The Rape of the Sabine Women,* contain elements of a narrative or a history. But to fully understand even those statements, there must be a title, a caption, or a commentary. To understand the neutrality of a photograph, consider what happens to the "meaning" if a photograph of a man holding a trapped fox appears in a trapping magazine or in a journal, say, for the Animal Liberation Front. In such cases, the photograph is not any new vision or slant. It is also an example of what the phenomenologists are fond of noting: that one's experience so "colors" what one sees, that much is frankly unavailable. One intends to see certain phenomena, and one seeks confirmation of that intention. And finds it.

The photo essay offers a way to extend one's coverage, but one is never going to "cover" a subject; or if he does, it will certainly be in an ironic way. Extending one's coverage can be simply presenting the subject in many different kinds of light or from different points of view. Such an organization helps to create a context, one that permits resonance, one that begins to comment upon itself. Merely multiplying the number of images does not necessarily promote greater vision or understanding. Less is often more. In this and certain other aspects, photographs share some common attributes with poems. Both tend to move in the direction of distillation. When is the proper concentration reached? This, of course, is debatable, but the artificer positions himself at a point where he hopes he will be able to make a discovery. And the discovery is wedded to the proper geometry. Something in the balance, the equipoise, of the subject, is recognized, realized.

Here the differences in a poem and a photograph become more problematic. As one reads a poem, he is moving through time. As he moves through time, he possesses the image of the world of the poem (not of the world). With a photograph, one does not move through time; at least, experiencing the photograph does not demand that one move through time in the same way one moves through it in a poem. It might be said that one is moving through space, the space of the photograph (not of the world), though it is apparent that a photograph may be "gestalted," its overall structure taken in at once, unlike that of a poem. But one's eye moves about the terrain of the photograph, homing in on provocative details: the size of the bear's tracks in the snow compared to those of the little fox; the great weight difference; the beauty and the threat contained in the ice and snow. As the eye moves across the landscape of the photograph, the mind may be urged to ponder many connections that are immanent in the frozen geometry. This is what moves—the mind moves toward and about the stasis of the work of art. Or, as Susan Sontag has put it: "The ultimate wisdom of the photographic image is to say: 'There is the surface. Now think—or rather feel, intuit—what is beyond it, what the reality must be like if it looks this way.' Photographs, which cannot themselves explain anything, are inexhaustible invitations to deduction, speculation, and fantasy."[4]

In a sense, one must bring more to a photograph than to a poem, because a photograph comes with less. That is, a poem brings with it a history bound in the very words themselves, a human achievement. The photograph—because it is so bound to the surface of the world, to the world of visible, reflected light—demands that one bring history to it. This, of course, is one reason why the majority of photographs appear with captions, or with text. The photographs are there to particularize, in a special way, the text and to offer an "eyewitness" authentication, as if to say this is no fictive art, this is "real."

It has been observed that taking a photograph of something or someone is a way of conferring importance on it. Someone being photographed by a couple of photographers suggests that something of interest is taking place. Even if it's a banal vacation shot, someone thought it was important enough to photograph. That someone singled out by framing a particular slice of space, a particular moment in time, from all the oceanic flux of the world, asserts an importance of some kind. For some subjects, however, the importance is felt by the photographer, and the subject has transcended this province. Taking a picture of the King of England surely does not add to his stature. And every member of our group would have, I think, agreed that the lord of the Arctic was beyond receiving any royal mantle from us. These bodies that are so much at the top of their scale, so awesome, so big, so powerful, left no doubt that it was the photographer and the viewer who were in the presence of importance. A view of Mt. Fuji, of Mt. Everest, of a three-thousand-year-old sequoia, all of these, given the human scale, somehow are not made more important. This is not to miss the initial point that a photograph can confer importance—especially upon some individual in a sea of humanity. But it is significant conversely to note that the power can go the other way.

Not only is photography a way of conferring importance, it is a way of violation, a way of predation. Nathaniel Hawthorne wrote that the greatest sin was the violation of the human heart. Notions of privacy have probably changed since he wrote that, even though the citizens may feel more violated or preyed upon because of the technical apparatus of the modern state (which includes photography). Even for those who might not give assent to a "soul" that will ascend to heaven, many do feel that there is yet something "inside" them that can be invaded and something vital that can be stolen. Predation is characterized as plundering, pillaging, victimizing for one's own gain.

The question arises, though, whether one can violate or plunder something or someone if it or he is not aware of the invasion taking place. I expect we would agree that children can be violated and not know it. Adults are in massive ways invaded by propaganda, but we tend to conclude that that's tough. When it comes to animals, no one seems to feel that any animal's privacy can be invaded. Without consciousness, we seem to have concluded, the notion of privacy is moot.

We find ourselves, however, at a curious place in the history of these attitudes and ideas. For the longest part of our history, we felt that the made image of something was a manifestation of its soul or spirit. A doll made to represent a god by a Hopi, a rock painting of a bison or a bear by Paleolithic man, was an avenue for influencing the presence, the spirit of the thing. An artist, or shaman-artist, was engaged in a pragmatic activity: that of either propitiating very powerful forces or gaining control in some way. To address the image was the same as addressing the thing itself.

But then, as Sontag so incisively points out, from at least Plato forward, the image became synonymous with *mere* appearance, and appearance was cut away entirely from the object depicted.[5] It is this divorce that separates us from the world of Paleolithic and Neolithic man—when the image participated in the reality of the subject, when the oil lamps were lit in the caves and in the flickering light the bison, the mammoth, the bear, and the deer were there.

Oddly, though, an unpredictable turn of events—or better, an unpredictable turn of mind—seems to have taken place. Photography, Sontag observes, has revived "—in wholly secular terms—something like the primitive status of images." The photograph is, in a sense, an extension of the very object by way of the reflected light, and achieves a "partial identity of image and object. . . . [T]he true modern primitivism is not to regard the image as a real thing; photographic images are hardly that real. Instead, reality has come to seem more and more like what we are shown by cameras."[6]

This is a profound change, if Sontag's observation is true, and I think it is. The multiplication of images has become so ubiquitous that the number of hours each day that the average Westerner spends receiving these selected versions of the world has thrown us into a precarious position. In the most obvious and immediate place, political and economic reality has more and more come to be the edited version of that reality prepared by a handful of people. Earlier, one might have been inclined to reply that he didn't know what was the truth or the reality about an event far beyond his ken. But now he is more likely to *believe* that he does know.

The results of image-inundation are manifold and certainly are felt in the perception of wild nature and of animals. One can easily delude himself into thinking he understands what it is like to "be out there" in the woods, or on the tundra, without being there. It's like thinking that one understands Mexico via a vacation poster. There is the illusion that one is participating in the world when instead he is residing in a reinforced world of solipsism and fantasy. The reinforcement is especially insidious because it rests solely on one sense, that of sight, at least once removed since what one is seeing is a photograph.

Why is this dangerous? Some delusions are worse than others. Ones that lead to political and economic expression can be disastrous, or at best quite misleading. One can seem to have appropriated the reality of animals by looking at beautiful pictures of them. Yet none of us thought that we had appropriated the polar bears as we lived near them and watched them. They were not to be possessed. And it is only another delusion to think that one has possessed or appropriated all aspects of the bear by killing him, skinning him, and breaking him down into smaller parts. One may analyze him (deconstruct him, freeze-frame him), but if one wants to know a polar bear on snow-covered tundra, one must look at a polar bear on snow-covered tundra.

What then about pictures of polar bears or hummingbirds? Are they only delusions of the worst kind? No. But they need to be considered in the same relation to the world as a map is to the Northwest Territories. To repeat Sontag's observation: "The ultimate wisdom of the photographic image is to say: 'There is the surface. Now think—or rather feel, intuit—what is beyond it, what the reality must be like if it looks this way.'"[7]

6

Finally, through the blowing snow the next morning, the light of a skidoo heralded Roy's return. With his rifle still strapped on his back, he looked like some Finnish or Russian winter soldier. After the general hooting and cheering, and his apologies for not getting back sooner, Roy described his trip to Churchill. He had made it to Knight's Hill and then broken down. He'd had to walk in to Churchill! Through a lot of bears, through subzero cold. At night. On his face were patch bandages where his face had been frozen.

Staring at Roy's partially frozen face and thinking about his long walk to Churchill reminded me of the champion walker out of Churchill, Samuel Hearne. An Englishman who left the Royal Navy quite young and joined the Hudson's Bay Company in 1769, Hearne had arrived at Fort Prince of Wales in Churchill that same year. Men were still looking for a shortcut to the Orient through the fabled Northwest Passage. The Company decided that a man should set out with the Indians and walk until he came to the Passage, or Strait of Anian. Samuel Hearne reached the fort around this time, and the head of the fort chose him to go. His first attempt in 1769 was to be a total flop. The Chipewyan Indians who went with him stole his supplies and deserted him. He was lucky to be able to walk back to the fort. He started out again on the Second Coppermine Expedition, so-called because Hearne found, additionally, the source of copper that there had already been some evidence of. It was February, the coldest month, and Hearne departed with five Indians, a small leather tent, and a gun—which is enough to boggle the mind. Just being out in −10°F now, helping Len and Roy fix the wheel, is bad enough. But there were light years of difference in setting out for a year or two with men you don't even know, for destinations that are unknown, with a tent and a gun. That was Hearne's lot, and it was to be a hungry lot. The men went seven days on cranberries, water, scraps of leather, and burned bones from old fires. Their stomachs shrank and when food was taken again they dared eat only "two or 3 ounces." Hearne's diary records, "I have frequently seen the Indians examine their wardrobe . . . and consider what part could best be spared." During the winter, of course, all the migratory birds that seem to cover the tundra are gone. Only the few amazing winter residents are left, and Hearne's group could catch only some of these for food. "Because of the long months of snow the ptarmigan were forever short of gravel for their crops and the Indians took advantage of this fact to catch them easily. They set up a pole, tied a net to it and baited the net with a heap of gravel. The grit-starved ptarmigan rushed for the net, the cord was yanked and the Indians piled on the flapping partridges and killed them by 'biting them at the back of the head.' With luck, three men could 'bite' three hundred birds in a forenoon."[8]

The Second Coppermine Expedition ended in failure too. Hearne's quadrant broke; Indians other than his fellow travelers robbed him of almost everything. But somehow he managed to walk back after nine months. He ran into an Indian chief, Matonabbee, who was to help him on his third attempt.

On the third expedition Hearne, Matonabbee (and women who accompanied them most the way), and a few other Chipewyans walked all the way to the Arctic Ocean! On the way, Hearne discovered for the Hudson's Bay Company the Coppermine River and the ore deposits. And by getting to the Arctic Ocean, he demonstrated that there was no Strait of Anian, or Northwest Passage. This time he was gone eighteen months and twenty-three days. There were no horses to carry their belongings and no food was taken with them. It was an incredible journey.

Right after unloading, Len took off with Roy to fix the snapped universal joint on the track vehicle. In just an hour, preceded by the skidoo, Len came down the esker like one of Rommel's men. Pulling up to the side of the Buggy where the wheel was loose, he then had the roof of the lower vehicle to hop up on in case the bears got too curious. Then we threw down sticks of spruce firewood. Len stacked them so that near the top they slanted beneath the huge axle. Then he had me "bump" the ignition with the transmission in reverse. Ever so slowly, with much adjustment and hammering of the top pieces of wood, the axle was raised just enough for the tire to be off the ground. It was one of the most ingenious, on-the-spot "shade tree" operations I had ever witnessed. It was this kind of creativity that caused all of us to hold Len in such high respect. And it is this kind of skill that is always supported by a native talent. One can certainly learn a great deal about mechanics. But anyone who has ever hung around a garage or an industrial shop is almost inevitably in the presence of someone who uses tools the way a Guidon Kremer uses the violin. It is a special way of seeing the world. Anyone can memorize certain mechanical procedures, but another kind of mind is required for seeing a machine, for example, laid out two-dimensionally, *or* the converse. Some women can look at a dress and see it laid out on the two-dimensional plane of fabric; others can't.

Submerged as we are in a technological age, many of us lose a sense of awe before the tool and, correspondingly, the mind that produced it. Only the showier tools like an Apollo moon vehicle get noticed. That is just one of the many reasons why people of the twentieth century need places to go that permit them to know where they came from. There is no way to go back as an unconscious animal (though we have all experienced people in national forests who come very close, but who in fact do not have the manners of wild animals). But that part of us that can go back unencumbered is refreshed. There follows a reciprocity of perspective. One of the consequences is to be able to obvert the tool and see it with respect, with awe. By reducing one's tool kit to basics, one is able to sense the elemental relationship it has with man. Forget your knife or your fire-maker and much is clarified. On the other hand, by carrying only the basic tools, one is thrown open to the natural, or nonartificial, world. Arctic and subarctic terrain especially conduce to this realization. Although there is much life in the Arctic, there is not as much life as in the tropics; the tropics have more species and more biomass. For this very reason it is easier to see the figurative *tree* instead of the overwhelming forest. Of course it is just trees that one doesn't see on tundra. But one has the heightened focus resulting from fewer species of plants and animals. Being alone on a vast tundra with only one's knife, fire-maker, and tent, like being alone at sea in a sailing vessel, reminds us of our marriage to the tool—its power and its embeddedness in *Homo sapiens sapiens*. To repeat a commonplace, there is no return to Eden, but in the attempt to return by hiking or camping in remote places, by sailing alone, Eden becomes clarified. What may occur to us finally is that we may not have been thrown out of Eden. We may have walked out, and been mostly glad we did.

Len's wooden jack was simple, yet ingenious enough to remind us of our audacious marriage to tools and how this marriage partner has changed us and our world. This is partly what Wallace Stevens would have us sense in his short poem "Anecdote of the Jar":[9]

I placed a jar in Tennessee,
And round it was, upon a hill.
It made the slovenly wilderness
Surround that hill.

The wilderness rose up to it,
And sprawled around, no longer wild.
The jar was round upon the ground
And tall and of a port in air.

It took dominion everywhere.
The jar was gray and bare.
It did not give of bird or bush,
Like nothing else in Tennessee.

Now I think Stevens' jar is not meant to be an especially happy event: it is gray and bare, and does not give of bird or bush. There is not only a power, but somehow a coerciveness, making the "slovenly wilderness/ Surround that hill." That particular sentiment is not the one I had in mind here, so much as the power of the difference in this manmade object and the wilderness. Also, the poem's linguistic landscape is not a thicket, but more a tundra. In such a simpler landscape, one is "refreshed." Not only is his animalness reaffirmed, but also his animalness with tools, walking east of Eden.

Finally, with much pounding and cursing, the huge wheel was shoved on the hub and fastened. There was a general sense of relief. Now we were back to not one, but two powered, movable vehicles. Since no bears were in the immediate vicinity, some of us piled into the smaller vehicle in order to replenish our sagging water reserves, but also just for a break-out from the close confines of our normal home. Of course, everything right near us was salt water. So we moved in a mile to one of the many tundra ponds. With the continued cold all the surfaces on shallow ponds had frozen. Running over other smaller patches of ice we discovered it was four or five inches thick. Len had brought his chain saw, and when we came to a likely spot he used it to cut a hole through the sheet of ice. Then we slowly filled up the plastic five-gallon containers.

After a bit, Bruemmer and I walked along the bank where there were some fairly heavy willows. He pointed to the small tracks of ptarmigan. Even though we saw another line of tracks, we did not see ptarmigan. What we did see was a line of fox tracks. Whether the fox had come along when the ptarmigan did, and whether he had been successful or not, we did not know.

Suddenly we saw two medium-sized bears trotting our way. They seemed to be trotting. They were trotting. But, boy, could they cover ground. With much hollering, we and the other men ran at high speed for the vehicle, with none of us taking an "after you" attitude. Once we were all inside, Len pulled back a portion of the plywood roof and stood up. The bears padded over, looking at us with the greatest curiosity. We returned the favor. As many people do in other circumstances, we looked into the eyes of the animal as if somehow we might be able to know what he was thinking, how he was feeling. There is a sense of trying to "cross over" as you stare into the eyes of bear, his head right before you. Soon one of them reared up, leaning against our little tank. It was then that it occurred to us that our thin-walled, plywood-covered tank is to bears much like barbed wire is to a cow. It's mostly the idea that keeps either from going through.

Our short gallop had Bruemmer breathing a little heavily. Len motions for one of Bruemmer's cigarettes. He was the only one of the ten of us who *brought* cigarettes. Len's announced intention was to quit smoking while he was out on this expedition. Unfortunately, Bruemmer had cigarettes and Len had a nicotine seizure. Or many. Slowly over the first week, Bruemmer's supply dwindled. Len never gave him any quarter. He bummed right to the end.

7

Another sunrise found us quietly eating our Red River Cereal, no doubt setting off paroxysms of childhood memories of innocence and simplicity, at least for Guravich. The rest of us spooned it reflectively, too. Then Bruemmer nudged me with his knee and motioned with his head. Right beside his right foot was the long gear shift, and where it disappeared into the floor the hole was covered with a rubber shield. It had been completely covered. Now a bear's snout was poking through! He had gnawed part of the shield away and was working on the rest. More evidence of the bear's love of synthetics. Bruemmer smacked him on the schnozz with his tablespoon and resumed eating. Our pest faded.

Bruemmer fell to musing about the time he had spent long days bear-watching in the nearby tower. One female came to be known as "Linda." She had been in Churchill before, had been tagged and numbered, and there was quite a record of her comings and goings. She had hung around the tower to become something of a pest for Bruemmer. He couldn't run her off very easily, and she stayed much on his mind. When he left Cape Churchill to return to his home and wife in Montreal, the memories of Linda were still very vivid. He said her name a few times in his sleep, endearingly and admonishingly, and his wife Maud asked who this woman was he had so much on his mind.

By the time we finished our cereal and cleaned up the dishes, the morning was all red with the early sun. The wind was gone, at least for a while; the bear under the Buggy had trudged out into the rosy landscape and our lenses were quickly snapped on, shutters clicking. As the sun was soon refracted by less atmosphere on its way up, the day turned crystalline. From across the esker the largest polar bear that we were to see came toward our bear under the Buggy. This new visitor was certainly over a thousand pounds. The other bears we saw were generally not in poor condition, according to the past experiences of Roy and Bruemmer. Still, they had been mostly scavenging for the last couple of months, having gone without their seal kills. This approaching bear had obviously found something. And a lot of it.

We quickly dubbed him "Magnum." It was not that he was particularly taller or longer than the other bears, but he was very wide, and the fat lay in large slabs all over his body. His head was as large as an old-fashioned washtub. Initially the smaller bear moved off; he knew he was no match and was deferring. There was no food or female to fight over, and thus no reason to run away. He was not bothering anybody. But Magnum padded over and raised a paw, inviting him to "play." Just being friendly. But the smaller bear was having none of it. He knew an uneven match-up when he saw one. So he moved away and eventually out of sight. Yet the etiquette had been observed. Magnum did not pursue him in annoyance. At no time for the remainder of our stay, did we see Magnum accepted in play. He sometimes appeared a lonely figure—much like the kid who wants to play football, but who is twice as big as his confederates.

Our leaning out the window a bit with our cameras drew Magnum over to the Buggy. He reared up on the side, his head reaching *almost* to where we were. He was a warrior; his face showed the old scars of earlier encounters of the violent kind. Looking over the side of the window only a foot from his face, I felt the power of his curiosity, his wonderment at what we were, at the meaning of such creatures as ourselves. Surely he would have eaten us, given the right set of circumstances, just as our own species, given the right circumstances, had eaten his. But at such a moment, when each of us considered the other, there was a powerful desire to reach beyond our separateness, as if the huge brown eyes of his massive head held the possibility of becoming the other, however briefly. His own cocked head seemed to express some reciprocal intent (of course, it could end up quite badly for me). Yet there was the gulf, this estrangement. The taking on of the animal could finally only be done by holding the idea of him in my head, by taking on what power, what inheritance he could pass on to me, as a spirit. Soon he gave up on the possibilities. We could not play-fight; we could not be eaten today; we were, finally, not his kind. And for one of the rare times, there was soon no bear on the scene.

As if to take the place of this recently departed spirit, came first one, then several, white wraiths, loping toward us, the white puff-balls of foxes. By now they associated us with food or food smells. Not wanting to use any more sardines than we had to, and also hoping that for a time the bears would stay away, we tried throwing crusts of bread out. And it worked. What looked like litter mates raced and competed for anything we tossed on the snow. Then from a little further to the east came several other foxes. As three more foxes moved closer, a member of the first litter ran toward them and snapped at the heels of one, who altered his course but was not going to be deterred. Bread or the occasional piece of ham was now hotly contested. If the scrap was large enough not to be eaten in one gulp, off the winner would go, sometimes pursued by his fellows.

They grew bolder and seemed to become so unafraid of us that Len eased down the front ladder. He stood very still with some bread in his outstretched hand. Feeling that his height was yet too threatening, Len lay on his stomach in the snow, hand still outstretched with bread—a whole roll, brought all the way from Milwaukee's bakeries by Treul. The boldest of the lot drew closer and closer, but not all at once. He was torn between his appetite for the huge Milwaukee roll and his fear of the giant figure lying in the snow, both seen for the first time. Like most of us, the fox let his appetite get the best of him. Stretching his neck as far as he could, he snatched the roll from Len's gloved hand and went tearing down the esker. His less courageous confreres had been watching the drama (like the men in the Buggy), and off they all went in hot pursuit. But, at least on this day, the spoils had gone to the quick and the brave.

Len's success only whetted all our appetites. At first, we went one at a time so as not to overwhelm these petite creatures; but as they grew accustomed more of us ventured out. It was hard to feed and photograph them at the same time. So Len, who was less interested in photography, kept them entertained. Finally, anyone who wanted to be was out in the bitter cold.

A hundred feet away two of the first litter were playing. One would come at the other with his tail raised, his back very arched, sidling or walking half-sideways toward the other. It seemed an invitation, like the gentle introductory cuffing of the bears. He nipped the other on the back legs and then off they would go, gliding over the crust of the snow.

Any time we left the immediate vicinity of the Buggy, where the tires or our earlier tramping around had crushed the snow, we would sink up to our knees. I finally found an unused "day bed" of a bear and stood in it. When I managed to entice a fox over to the edge of the day bed with a piece of bread, if I were kneeling, he was at face level. At such times, there is a magic excitement at being so close and among creatures that are meeting humans for the first time. It drives home the point that others have made before, that the fugitive and little-seen animals near man's towns and near the hunter's guns behave differently than they did when first they encountered men who did not hunt them. Or this seems to be true for some animals at least.

Several of us had motor drives for our cameras, and wearing thick gloves it was difficult to have full control over the shutters. But with the gloves off, our hands came close to freezing. And the cameras did freeze up, in a very short time. The batteries couldn't take much of this kind of cold. Of course we used silver-oxide batteries in the cameras themselves, but the batteries that drove other parts of the system would go down. We had to take them back into the Buggy, which was fairly cold itself, but seemed a relative sauna.

Being out in the cold with the foxes reminded me of their striking adaptation to cold. After all, they had to be able to make it in $-94°F$. They have perhaps the longest body hair of any arctic animal (certainly in relation to their small size). With such insulation, even at $-94°$, their metabolic rate only goes up 37 percent! To give that some perspective, a naked man doubles his at $64°F$ and triples it at $45°F$.

They have only just gotten their white coats. The arctic fox molts twice a year, which in itself is a considerable expenditure of energy. Around early April he begins to lose his white coat; and by June his face, legs, and upper body are covered with short, brown, summer fur, his body's underside a yellowish brindle. Obviously this change is not related to heat conservation. If it were, he would do like man and wear white linen in summer and dark wool in winter. One assumes the fox's changes represent protective coloration.

All the arctic foxes we saw were white, but the species is dimorphic. In some coastal areas a blue "morph" is principally what is seen, though this was not true here. Bruemmer remarks that the blue phase seems to predominate around areas where there are bird cliffs, and there are no bird cliffs around Cape Churchill. But there are hundreds of thousands of birds during the summer nesting season—not only the thousands of snow geese that nested at La Pérouse Bay, but the thousands of other birds that nest on the tundra, their eggs and young ready victims of our little foxes.

Suddenly our fun and freezing outside the Buggy came to an abrupt halt. Across the frozen pools behind the beach came two yellow-white male bears heading our way, so we scrambled back inside. Although they did not appear to be running, they covered the ground with amazing rapidity. They had hustled over, no doubt, out of curiosity. Or maybe because of the smells the Buggy was putting off. The foxes didn't leave, though; they just kept loping and circling.

The bears drew up at a spot in the snow that had had *muktuk* on it, and they went to licking the icy snowball. One of the foxes came darting in and one of the big males roared at him, chasing him forty or fifty feet before he would return. The fox didn't seem to be bothered in the least, but just kept circling. One bear lay on his stomach to lick the snow without standing, his feet stretched out behind him like some sunbather. His companion was licking his paw where the juices or smells of the *muktuk* had stuck. He seemed very delicate, even fastidious. With both of the bears concentrating so intently, the foxes became more confident, moving ever closer, until one daring white raider actually went up to the bear on the ground and licked his back paw! A cheer went up among the men at his audacity.

The arctic fox must have audacity, or at least be driven by powerful survival instincts to make it through most winters. His principal food is the lemming. In the winter, the lemming, who does not hibernate like the ground squirrel, is insulated and hidden by the warm blanket of snow. Under this blanket he feeds on mosses and the standing bases of grass and sedge; he uproots their rhizomes. In his feeding he makes a maze of tunnels underneath. In his moving about, he sometimes betrays his presence and the arctic fox has a chance, but only a chance, to break the snow crust and grab the lemming. But the advantage is to the lemming in winter, because he has so many places to hide and the fox can't dig up the whole tundra. Even the bears will try to reach a lemming or a ground squirrel. In summer I have seen whole ground squirrel networks ravaged, though it's much like using a giant bulldozer to dig a flower garden. The bear-calories expended in getting a lemming don't seem worth it.

Much has been written about lemming population cycles. The individual lemming life is very brief in human terms. The collared lemming, for example, may live, if he is lucky, a year. But one authority has estimated that 30 percent of the population dies every two weeks. With their rapid breeding (five or six litters a year), they not only maintain a viable breeding population, they far exceed it, which ultimately leads to collapse.

The smallest of arctic herbivores, the lowly lemming is of great interest to arctic ecologists. After all, it is a very important part of the food chain. Some of the mystery of the lemming's population cycles has become clearer in recent years. It may be that weasel predation during critical times in winter, when there is also some reproduction, may be more important than reductions by summer predators (including weasels). If the weasels went south in the winter, like the rough-legged hawks and the long-tailed jaegers, the lemming would have a much easier time of it. His population might surge more frequently. The biological kismet might be the same, however, because when the lemming is very abundant, so are the snowy owls, the rough-legged hawks, the jaegers. And, of course, so are our little white foxes. Yet we are reminded again of the marriage between predator and prey. When the lemmings are few, so are the foxes. And that is one reason the foxes are found far out on the ice following the lord of the arctic. If the bear is skillful—and lucky—he will kill plenty of seals and have enough left over for his followers.

While all this was going on, Fred Treul dropped one of the lenses of his glasses out the window, somewhere in the snow. It was the only pair he had. Bruemmer dashed down the front ladder and managed to find it and get back in before any of the bears came over. But one had moved swiftly over toward us—again, out of interest. There was some clucking of disapproval from Guravich about this, but Treul was grateful to get his lens back.

Following that brief episode, the world turned red again and the light failed rapidly. After all our running around outside with the foxes, the Muktukers were happy to commence their cocktail hour. Bruemmer was by now joining us, as was Treul. Earlier in the week, in response to Guravich's query about who owned the bottle of Dubonnet standing among his cooking things, I opined that it must be Len's (who was off somewhere in the track vehicle). "Got to be Len's," I said. "He's all the time mixing up his sweet concoctions." Bruemmer, who was standing nearby, finally realized we were talking about his one bottle of libation, and he fell to instructing me about the exquisiteness of his aperitif.

8

If you come to a place for the first time, you might well speak of such coming as "exploring." But to explore the poles for the first time is unlike exploring New Orleans, for example. If there is no one to tell you how to go, if there are no other humans, the sense of the unknown is vastly greater. In this place that for so long was really unknown, the Arctic and Subarctic easily call to mind men who had no one to tell them where or how to go. Like Samuel Hearne, Jens Munk was such a voyager, and his spirit still walks the land. If one knows how to call him up. Ever since reading the diary of this Danish sea captain and explorer, I have been haunted by his spirit, especially when I am around Hudson Bay. It was because of my own knocking about the western shores of the Bay that I became interested in him. After all, one wants to know what spirits have come before so that, as the spirits to come, we may comport ourselves properly.

His king had sent him on one of those numerous quests for the Northwest Passage. He sailed with two ships, as the commander of the expedition: he skippered the larger *Unicorn* and the other ship was the *Lamprey*. When they finally set sail, there was a total complement of sixty-five men. By the time their brave and horrible story was over, only three returned. Theirs is one of the great stories of human endurance, and of human pain and despair.

In the fall of 1619 they had come to the western shore of the Bay, the ice obviously ready to lock them in for the winter. They fortunately found the mouth of the Churchill River where their ships would have a better chance of surviving. Already there was a little sickness, and scurvy would soon set in with a vengeance. But in September, Munk's spirits were high. On September 12, he writes: "In the morning early, a large white bear came down to the water near the ship, which stood and ate some Beluga flesh, off a fish named which I had caught the day before [the Beluga whale]. I shot the bear, and the men all desired the flesh for food, which I also allowed. I ordered the cook just to boil it slightly and then to keep it in vinegar for a night, and I myself had two or three pieces of this bear-flesh roasted for the cabin. It is of good taste and did not disagree with us."[10]

Some of these bears outside our Buggy, curled up for their nap and partly out of the wind, may be that bear's descendants. He was, as far as I know, the first bear of Churchill written about. His initial meeting with a white man was not particularly felicitous. But his body was not wasted.

The brutal winter of Churchill in 1619 had not yet started to take its toll two months later. "On the 10th of November, which was St. Martin's Eve, the men shot some ptarmigan, with which we had to content ourselves, instead of St. Martin's goose; and I ordered a pint of Spanish wine for each bowl to be given to the men, besides their daily allowance; wherewith the whole crew were well satisfied, even merry and joyful."[11]

In the course of our talking about Jens Munk on this St. Martin's Eve, Len discovered that I had never eaten ptarmigan.

"Never? Never eaten ptarmigan?" he asked incredulously, as if it covered the earth. I think he wanted the excuse to move around as much as he wanted to get me a ptarmigan. But he set out in the track machine with his .22, confident he would have a table full by nightfall, which was only a couple of hours away.

After Len had gone, Guravich took out chickens to thaw. "Don't you have any faith in Len's skill?" asked somebody jokingly.

"He knows I don't like that. I've told him," said Guravich, clucking around his long cooking table, rearranging some of his implements.

"You mean shooting a ptarmigan or eating a ptarmigan?"

"There's just no sense in it," he replied, not really answering the question.

When Len returned, he had one ptarmigan. He felt profoundly perplexed. "I've never gone out and not gotten more than this. I don't understand it. I saw signs everywhere." Fred, Roy, and I had jumped to the ground next to his vehicle. There in the cold we examined the beautiful feathers of this member of the grouse family.

"We got both kinds around Churchill," commented Roy. "Rock and willow." This was a willow, without the splash of black from the bill to the eye. The genus name, *Lagopus,* reflects the interesting characteristic of densely feathered legs—*lagos* meaning hare, *pous* meaning foot, thus hare-footed. This feathering increases during the winter. A further adaptation is the claws. In winter they are almost twice as long as in summer. This creates a snowshoe effect, enabling them to make it through soft snow in their search for willow catkins and twigs when food is so hard to find. Such birds are quite remarkable when one considers that they may survive at 40° below zero.

Another adaptation of the ptarmigan is similar to that of the arctic fox. Both turn white in winter and are, thus, less vulnerable to predators. Come warm weather and snow melt, the ptarmigan changes to mostly summer brown. Interestingly, Bruemmer points out, the male retains his telltale white longer than the female and remains more vulnerable during the beginning of the nesting season. In his *Encounters with Arctic Animals,* Bruemmer has written that "Nature, it seems, has assigned the cock ptarmigan a sacrificial role. While the female in drab summer dress sits quietly on the nest, the cock, white and extremely conspicuous, perches on a nearby rock, an inviting target for any foraging falcon or fox. Studies have shown predators at this time take primarily male ptarmigan. Thus die the proud little cocks, while the hens raise undisturbed the next generation of ptarmigan."

The bird felt as if it weighed about a pound before Len cleaned it. Finished, we all hurriedly climbed back up the front door ladder. Everyone had been casting eyes in all directions for bears.

Inside Guravich, having decided to cook chicken and spaghetti, had a big pot with cut-up pieces of chicken and a tomato sauce, lots of chopped onions, bell peppers (these, like most fresh vegetables and fruits this far north, worth their weight in gold), and seasoned with some oregano. And garlic, of course. When Len took his bird and started cutting it in several pieces, Guravich asked, "What are you doing? What are you going to do with that?"

"Might as well throw it in with the chicken. Didn't get enough for a meal."

"But we have plenty of chicken," he replied, clearly pained.

"Yeah, I know, but I promised Mills some ptarmigan. He's never eaten any." And he went on chopping, oblivious to or unwilling to note the undercurrent.

As the chicken (and ptarmigan) simmered away in the Buggy, the rest of us trooped back to the Muktuk Saloon. After we mixed our first aperitifs I fell to thinking about the curious stance of Guravich and others like him regarding hunting. Such people are not rejecting the ptarmigan on the grounds of the aesthete or the gourmet—that would, of course, be a matter of taste. They are rejecting the ptarmigan on the basis of ethics. They believe that it is wrong to eat the game bird.

Now one doesn't find, say, certain Buddhist attitudes against the eating of any animal as inconsistent with their metaphysics. One may or may not want to argue the metaphysics, but at least refusing to eat flesh is consistent with their vision. What we are discussing, though, is someone who can easily (and with gusto) eat a chicken that was perhaps raised in southern Canada, killed by someone there, then shipped all the way north to be eaten, but cannot eat a member of the same family, after killing it in northern Manitoba.

Somehow the inconsistency of Guravich's stance suggests a turning away of some sort. Is it a fastidiousness of the spirit? Why does someone so forcefully revolt against eating ptarmigan and not chicken? Put that way, the matter seems banal at best, trivial at least. The turning away, perhaps, is a turning inward, a vicariousness, a narcissism. But how does one account for the "callousness" of eating the chicken? I suspect it has to do with the general shift of the population from rural areas to urban ones. With that shift several experiences have changed dramatically. Growing up, one simply does not see a lot of births in the lives of animals, or a lot of deaths. Birth and death are much more hidden. Human babies do not arrive at home, but in a distant hospital. People die and are quickly whisked out of sight. The trajectory of life is broken up so that the fact of its trajectory is denied. What death one might happen upon in large cities, the experience of it, is somehow contravened by its violent nature, its "unnatural" cause. Thus death itself seems unnatural.

Such contradictions were noticed by Chaucer in his Prioress, the nun riding along with the other Canterbury pilgrims. Here is a woman who has formally dedicated herself to otherworldliness. But she is described as a mannered though committed gourmet and a lusty drinker who decorates herself with beads and a golden brooch. Although she weeps if she sees a mouse caught in a trap, she feeds her small hounds with roasted flesh. She is "all conscience and tender heart," but she ends up telling one of the most violent tales in the book.

Growing up in Winnipeg, Guravich had never been a hunter, though he is a committed and accomplished gardener, and a committed eater of flesh. But he was a tank commander in the Canadian army during World War II. Perhaps that experience holds the key to his attitude about killing something oneself. In the play-fighting of the men in the Muktuk Saloon, though, because he had been a tank commander and because of the way he ran his kitchen and remained relatively aloof during the evenings, Guravich ultimately became known as Herr Panzerkommandant.

Later in the evening as we sat down to eat, Len triumphantly placed the steaming bird on my plate. It did not taste exactly like chicken—it was a denser meat. But it tasted good, and confirmed that I was in a different place.

9

The hunting of the ptarmigan (and the eating of the ptarmigan) sets up resonances with the matter of taking the picture of ptarmigan or eider ducks or polar bears. The two activities at some points seem to be related; the context of the activities seems to be the same; and at critical points, there are oppositions. One of the few serious inquiries into the nature, function, and ethics of hunting is Ortega y Gasset's "Meditations on Hunting." This first appeared as a substantial introduction to a book entitled *Twenty Years a Big-Game Hunter* by his friend Edward, Count Yebes, which was published in Madrid in 1943.

The very bringing together in one place of hunter and photographer, or hunting and photography, can reveal conflicts of taste, of ethics, and of the very way one looks at the world. Often, however, the hunter and photographer may be found in the same person, though not at the same time. All but two of our group had been hunters, or were still. The only two who had not hunted were reared in strictly urban areas. It is a fact, however, that one who hunts may choose to photograph the animal, or the photographer may choose instead to hunt. I say this, because Ortega pummels photography in a way that I think reveals other concerns and objections. Sometimes I think he may have been settling certain debts he had with some Englishmen as he shaped some of his remarks. For example:

> The English have initiated a form of hunting in which all these conflicts of conscience are cleverly eluded: it is a matter of having the hunt end, not with the capture or death of the animal, but rather with taking the game's picture. What a refinement! Don't you think so? What tenderness of soul these Anglo-Saxons have! One feels ashamed that one day, at siesta time thirty years ago, one killed that overly impertinent fly! Of course the British Empire was not forged with silks and bonbons, but by employing the greatest harshness Western man has ever seen in the face of the suffering of other men.[12]

He accuses the English (and, by inference, those engaged in photographic hunting) of mannerism and ethical mandarinism—of a new immorality "which is a matter of not knowing those very conditions without which things cannot be. This is man's supreme and devastating pride, which tends not to accept limits on his desires and supposes that reality lacks any structure of its own which may be opposed to his will."[13] This is, at bottom, what is critical: the recognition that zoological life depends on the death of other life. And any kind of mannered evasion of this is unserious, though that does not mean it is harmless. It is of the order of delusion when one lives as if he has not heard of death; it is possible to "get by" often, but such a position abrogates any authentic meaning to one's existence. It is, in short, a fool's paradise.

Does this mean that one must hunt to be authentic? Of course not. The hunter-gatherer, after some six hundred thousand years, managed to figure out a more dependable, safer way of keeping animals in order to kill them when he needed them. And perhaps more often than not, thereafter, he endured life with less peril. It likely was the hunter-gatherer's adaptation to the world that led to, as Paul Shepard has written, "the specialization of some parts of the central nervous system for storing and transmitting information symbolically."[14] Without this specialization, no agriculture, and perhaps less leisure to think about matters, though the latter is more debatable (hunters may have had considerable leisure). Yet, if ritual and history have any meaning, surely the reenactment of 99 percent of that human past is not insignificant. Those who choose to hunt take part in an activity of the mind *and* body in its reenactment. Anyone who is shortsighted enough to feel embarrassed by 99 percent of his upbringing, of what it is to be human, is an embarrassment himself. No, one obviously does not have to hunt, in the same way that he is not forced to read history or consider myths or look at cave art, but his life will surely be less the feast it might otherwise have been.

Because one cannot (or will not) see the processes that furnish him with the very basis for his physical existence, he is wide open for the estranged condition that twentieth-century man finds himself in—locked off in a section of some production line within which he does not know where things are coming from or toward where (or for what reason) they are going away. And he comes not to care. Then he generalizes on the basis of his one cell or one section. If there is a way out of the cell, it is a poverty not to take it, if only on occasion, in order to know one's relation to the whole.

Paul Shepard writes in the same introduction to the Ortega y Gasset essay:

> Now we are ready to find in our heads the mind of the hunter: the development of human memory as a connecting transformer between time and space, derived from the movement of hunter and gatherer through a landscape; the Dionysian moment of unity and freedom in ecstasy of intense release unknown to herbivores, based on the recognition of the perpetuation of life at the moment of the kill; the mental use of other species as metaphors for social perception, which is a mode of totemic transformation reaching to the heart of thought, yoked by our evolution to the richness of world life, ushered into consciousness by the magic of the taxonomies of the species system and the terminology of anatomy as revealed by the hunter as butcher.[15]

With the coming, by fits and starts, of consciousness, of flashes of reason, the impact, the repercussion, of this event—the perpetuation of life at the moment of the kill—upon Pleistocene man was manifold and generative. For this likely led to the demand for propitiating the spirits of the animals upon whom he had committed this outrage. It may well be a fruitful speculation to consider that this Dionysian moment of release and recognition has led to art and religion as well. Surely it is consciousness, and especially the consciousness of death, that leads to both.

And what is hunting? This, of course, is what Ortega spends some 150 pages trying to get at. He insists that one must not confuse that which has to do with hunting and hunting itself. Whether it be utilitarian hunting or sports hunting is incidental. Even the poacher's hunting. And he says that "killing is not the *exclusive* purpose of hunting." He includes capturing the animal for several purposes. But there is a boundary, resulting from the confrontation of animal and hunter, beyond which hunting is no longer hunting. The hunter crosses the boundary "just at the point where man lets loose his immense technical superiority"—such as poisoning a stream, which would be an overwhelming superiority in weapons.

Too, one must recognize, Ortega continues, that "hunting occurs throughout almost the entire zoological scale." And in all cases, there is an agent, the hunter, and a subject, the hunted. These are not two creatures who have confronted each other to fight. That would be mutual aggression. But that is not what hunting is. With these qualifications and exclusions, Ortega defines hunting as "what an animal does to take possession, dead or alive, of some other being that belongs to a species basically inferior to its own. Vice versa, if there is to be a hunt, this superiority of the hunter over the prey cannot be absolute."[16] Even when the vastly larger polar bear seeks to hunt a lemming, the lemming has a chance to evade the hunter, and in fact is often successful in this evasion.

When Ortega accuses "photographic hunting" of evasion, he means then that it evades "certain ultimate requirements without which the reality 'hunting' evaporates." And it is hard for us to evade Ortega's argument. There is some problem with his definition. That is, if it includes taking possession of a live animal, has one engaged the serious matter of zoological life depending on death (does any animal except man do this?)? Yet this quibble will not overthrow the main point. And for him, the main point is that "all of hunting becomes spectral when a photographic image, which is an apparition, is substituted for the prey."[17] Spectral. Ultimately Ortega accuses photographic hunting of cheating the instinct. We attempt to satisfy its demand of something tangible to capture with the captured image of an animal—a view of the animal, an idea of it. By mocking the instinct to capture the animal, we lead to its atrophy, its demise. By coming away with only the apparition, an idea, we create and perpetuate a divorce, an estrangement, from the world.

I think another way to consider the matter might be to make it clear that photography is not hunting. Merely because it has been called "photographic hunting" need not lead us astray. It never was hunting. This misnaming may have been merely a travel agent's ploy. It was a predictable progression, for animal photography involves many activities that are similar to those that accompany hunting. One goes to the same terrain, has similar camping equipment, endures the good or bad weather. Yet the *intention* was never to hunt. What makes the matter complicated, of course, is that the language has been taken over by photography: to "capture" the animal on film, "to get a shot of it." One is going to try to "capture" or possess the animal in another way.

Paradoxically, trying to possess the animal by making a picture of it recalls the Paleolithic cave artist who tried to do the same. But unlike the cave artist, who felt his image was a real manifestation of the animal's spirit, we do not.

Of course, taking pictures is different from viewing pictures. None of us saw any of our photographic images until we left the scene. No one was using Polaroid. And the photographer looking at his own pictures is capable of filling in a mass of experiential detail surrounding the image. He may not even be able to "see" the image as pure image in the way that a stranger might. Correspondingly, the image is less pure apparition, but perhaps serves more as a rosarial device. That, of course, is partly why someone's vacation pictures are never as interesting to others as they are to the one who took them. The photographer himself is less vulnerable to the illusion that he has appropriated reality than is someone who has only the information that the photograph conveys. As others have pointed out, it is an illusion, this seeming to appropriate or possess reality.

No, photography is not hunting. There is never the possession that is possible in hunting. When Len went out to hunt for the ptarmigan, he would possess the world in a fundamental way (as would I when I ate it). Whether because all of the senses are involved (whereas only a single one is involved in a photograph) or because something basic to the structure of human existence has been touched, what is possessed or known is wider and deeper.

IO

This early morning before the sun was really above the rim of the world, we saw the most pathetic of bears, whom we finally dubbed "Old Bones." Roy thought he had seen the same bear last year, and he'd felt sure that last winter would be the final time he would see him. In this cold, with the snow particles swirling by at perhaps fifteen knots, Old Bones looked very much like some aged veteran fallen on hard times, huddled on a Chicago street, hoping to last out Lake Michigan's blasts. Unlike the other bears, he had not had a good summer. His ribs showed through; his head and gaunt neck listed to the side as if it were too much effort to face straight ahead. He looked as if the next blast of wind would tumble him over. Obviously he was not feeling the cold as we would have been feeling it. Yet it was hard not to believe that he wasn't. It is so tempting to project our feelings onto animals and then receive the emotional echo that confirms them.

In another demonstration of bear etiquette, the younger but mature bears seemed to leave him alone, to defer to him. If he lay down, they would walk around him so as not even to appear threatening. They acted as if they knew that it was not the proper thing to go up and offer to play-fight. As he moved ever so slowly, it was clear that he was stiff in his joints, that if bears had arthritis he had it. We were left to wondering whether he would still be able to move swiftly enough to kill his seals this winter. Out of this sense of pity, someone threw a sardine in his direction. Other bears were nearby. It was with some surprise that we watched him move with such alacrity and with a muffled roar to ward off those much heavier. Not that they would have refused to compete for the food. But when Old Bones was finished making his moves, and making the most of them, he resumed his lethargic, energy-saving quietude.

Following breakfast Len thought it would be useful to burn the garbage that could be burned. There was an old oil drum at the base of the tower that had been used for that purpose by the wildlife researchers. We moved all our camera gear to the Buggy and detached from the Muktuk, our cave of warmth and high bear talk. The bears stayed where they were, or else moved off for something more interesting. None followed us along the esker.

We welcomed the opportunity to get out and move around, and everyone pitched in with the burning. It wasn't long, however, before Bruemmer started urging, "Len, Len." Len looked where Bruemmer was pointing. Over a rise in the tundra a mother and cubs were coming slowly in our direction. Everybody scrambled up the ladder. Dan urged Len to move the Buggy over where we would have a better background for our shots, perhaps on both sides of the vehicle. When Len started up, at first the mother stopped and looked as if we had scared her, but soon we were silent once more, everyone making the effort not to let the windows down with a clatter.

On she came, but not with any speed. Over and over she raised her nose to the world of telltale scents. Maybe the smoke, so out of place in the clean air of the north, had drawn her. Unlike the smell of smoke on the southern prairies, there was no danger of a death-trapping fire here. Of course, by now the smell of heated sardines was wafting toward her and the cubs, setting up the great conflict: life-sustaining food or maybe the death-threatening strangeness of the weird machine on the esker. The sardines won.

She was so nervous. And the twin cubs were mostly so oblivious to the dangers in their icy world. Maybe she could feel all the excitement in the Buggy; if it is possible to transmit any kind of energy, electrical or otherwise, by concentration and direction, she must have felt the megawattage of awe, reverence, and chills of pure luck coming from us—like what you feel when your horse comes across the line first. Despite our enormous care, still the occasional creak or scratch sounded to her across the few feet of snow, and she would act to go away, would lift her elegant head and try to sniff some micro-trace of danger, all the while being bombarded by sardine. Her Bobbsey twins of innocence ambled forward like, "Well, you gotta expect old folks to be conservative . . . what do they know?"

Their story likely began around May of the year before when their mother mated with one of the vigorous males out on the ice. Their eggs lay dormant, though, until around September when they implanted themselves in the walls of her uterus. About this time last year, while the males and infertile females waited to go out on the ice, she instead headed south of here to a denning area. There she dug herself a snow den, and around late December or January her cubs were born. Most of the mothers seem to den around the Owl River Basin. There they try to find a slope of some kind, sometimes a riverbank, but a place where the snow collects. Usually she digs in a few feet and then upward for the chamber. Sometimes there is a second "room." The main room is on average 5′ × 7′ and 3′ high. She also makes a ventilation hole. It is conjectured that the female alters the size of the hole as she needs to regulate the temperature inside. She may also regulate the level of snow above the den by scraping.

The babies are born hairless and blind, weighing the grand sum of a pound and a half. They remain in the den with her until break-out, which occurs between early February and early April. By this time they weigh on average twenty pounds. Investigators who have looked at the dens once the family leaves have noted their cleanliness. Russian researchers have observed that females may leave the den very briefly to clean themselves. Little fecal matter is found in the den. Traces of urine are very rare. Recently physiologist Ralph Nelson has discovered, while testing black bears in Colorado, that they are turning their metabolic waste products into food. Instead of passing urea, the poisonous by-product of protein metabolism, out through the urine (as they do in summer), they convert the urea back into protein. Whether this is true of polar bears is not yet known.

After the mother breaks out of the den, the cubs spend their time like puppies, frolicking, chasing each other, and already beginning to develop the agility and strength they will soon need to survive. After this interval, the slow rest-and-go trek to the ice on Hudson Bay begins. There is still maximum ice cover, and the sealing is still good. But rather than merely kill for one's self, like the males, the mother must provide for the three of them. Not only must she feed them, she has also to defend them against males who just might want to cause trouble. One of the funniest sights is a cub racing around as if the whole Arctic were his exclusive province when suddenly a giant male comes trotting over. Off skedaddles the cub behind his mother, whereupon she has to do any fighting that will be done. Generally she will try the sensible tactic of avoiding trouble, but if the shoot-out comes, she will fight ferociously to defend her babies.

The family out our windows now was bathed in gold. These bears were yellow-white anyway, and with the angle of light, the trio and the winter sedges they stood in came together in a vortex of the world one always seeks.

Finally the spell broke. The air must have seemed loaded with threats for her and her cubs. Slowly she walked away, the terrible responsibility of a parent straddling her like her fur.

We turned back toward our own tiny house. Taking a slightly different route, but still along the esker, we came upon what was left of a skeleton. Roy said it was bear and the circumstances of the death were not clear. It had happened last year. Whether the bear was killed by one of its own or whether it died, he was not sure. That carnivory followed was likely.

Back in the Muktuk later my thoughts about the remains of the bear skeleton on the esker brought to mind older bear bones seen in pictures. Bones found all the way back through the Pleistocene are an important reminder of what the bear meant to man when man came along as man. I think of those at Montespan and Tuc d'Audoubert in France. In Montespan there is a roughly modeled headless bear, nearly a yard long. Observers theorize that the real bear's skull found between the forelegs was originally attached to the body by a wooden peg. Perhaps a bear skin had been wrapped around the statue. In the various animal statues one finds holes that presumably are the results of spears having been thrown at them.

All over the Neanderthal world, arrangements of bear skulls and bear bones have been found in caves. In Regourdou, France, the body of a brown bear was buried in a trench and covered with a very large stone. In Drachenloch, Switzerland, a stone cist was built and bear skulls were stacked inside. In Petershöhle Cave in Bavaria, ten bear skulls were placed on a platform. What was the meaning of this for Neanderthal man? Obviously it is impossible to know for sure. But they would hardly have gone to the trouble of burying and placing an 850-kg stone over a bear if it had only been a "trophy."

To arrive at even a probable answer one must try to imagine man as he passes from the world of the purely animal to that of *Homo sapiens,* passes over long corridors of time that are almost as hard to hold in mind as the oceanic eons of astronomical time. We must try imagining this long world in view of the facts that we have. It is needless to attempt to describe the flurry of paleontological activity that has been going on the last forty or fifty years: Dart's, the Leakeys', Johannson's, and White's. But that man made his way to man on the shoulders of the ape is now beyond reasonable doubt. Demand any more rigor of analysis than has been expended and you stop all dialogue.

In his brilliant *The Eternal Present: The Beginnings of Art,* Sigfried Giedion has carried out speculations that have to do with this transition of animal to man. Giedion observes that very early man considered himself *a minor creature.* After all, as he turned to the protein of large animals, how could he not realize his own relative smallness? How could he fail to acknowledge that he was less powerful personally than a mammoth, a lion, a bison?

As we try to imagine the life of this minor creature we remember that the world prior to agriculture was eminently "zoomorphic." Man had not yet reached the conclusion that he was the master of creation. Giedion suggests that it is difficult for us to comprehend, to fully recall the great duration of time that bound man to animal, and bound him in an intensely intimate relationship. Not only the knowledges of pursued and pursuer, of stalker and stalked bound them, but the intimate knowledge of taking the prey animal within one's self: a "Take, eat, this is my body," a reminder that one's very life depends on this "taking in," this devouring of a life, this killing of the sacred one.

Thus, since man was on such intimate terms with animals, felt himself less powerful than his prey individually, no wonder he displayed such an intensity of feeling by the time he was showing this in his cave art in 20,000 B.C. No wonder he went to such great trouble to make the scaffolding to reach the ceilings of the cave, or lit the fatty lamps that gave him the flickering, magical light to draw and paint and etch these animals in the rock and clay.

Consciousness was very likely a developing, changing capability of man. For whatever reason that the circuitry in our brains found its way to consider itself, found its way to factor time and consider what went before and what would come, there must have been an ebbing and flowing of consciousness, just as there is today. Sometimes we are conscious of part of what we are doing and often we are not. Perhaps prehistoric man's periods of consciousness were much less frequent in the beginning than now (and perhaps future men may be much more than we are). And there are different scopes of consciousness. When we are driving across the tundra, taking in its sweep and talking about it, that's one kind; when we point our cameras, sharply focusing our attention, tunneling our awareness, that's another kind; or when we stop nearly all physical activity, assume a lotus position and meditate, making a special attempt to "be aware," that's another. Clearly there exist many species of consciousness.

As the undulating curtain of self-consciousness–unself-consciousness shifted and *Homo sapiens* seemed to "stand outside himself" (a doppelgänger effect, a soul), so did he consider the animals, plants, and the constituents of the inorganic world to have souls. And these souls were all about. They were about in the daylight world, just as they were clearly about in the night world of dream. These spirits or souls were there somewhat the way they are there for many even today, spirits who can watch them, spirits with whom they speak—except that the invisible and the visible were then so much more closely united.

The attitude of primitive man toward the sacred is instructive here. Quoting anthropologist A. R. Radcliffe-Brown's 1945 lecture on religion and society, Giedion writes that the sacred was "connected with the concept of *taboo,* a word derived from the Polynesian *tabu,* meaning simply 'to forbid,' 'forbidden.' This includes the prohibition of touching in any way. . . . The sacredness of a chief and 'the uncleanness' of persons put to death for sinning against a taboo are denoted by the same word: *tabu.*" Giedion observes further that "this ambivalence is merely another form of the interlocking of visible and invisible. A single cord unites the heights and depths. Animals are simultaneously objects

Arctic fox in a blue snowscape

Bears often stand
to see farther

A gathering of bears

Cutting our water

The Tundra Buggy and
the Muktuk Saloon

A bear in his day bed

Staying close to Mama

Jousting in
the straw

133

Ringed seals ready to dive

Eskimo skinning a ringed seal

Study in blue

Sunset

of adoration, life-giving food, and hunted quarry. Many rites for the pacification and propitiation of the slain animal are known from the latest stages of the age of the hunter."[18] There is the double significance of the animal as object of worship and as a source of nourishment.

Totemism reflects this interlocking of the fates of man and animal, or for that matter the whole world. The animal had not yet been overthrown, or dethroned. To arrive at some idea of how primitive man felt toward animals, psychologists suggest a similarity with children. Freud writes, "Children show no trace of the arrogance which urges adult civilized men to draw a hard-and-fast line between their own nature and that of all other animals. Children have no scruples over allowing animals to rank as their full equals."[19]

There are several expressions of totemism: direct descent from an animal, a close relationship between one's primeval ancestor and a revered animal, and the interchange of forms (the animal becoming a man or a man taking on the form of an animal). Although we may never be absolutely certain, Giedion writes that "the representations upon the cavern walls give certain indications that the origin of totemism was rooted in the relations of man-animal, animal-man. The closest connections appear in creatures which combine both man and animal within one being."[20]

So we envision a world where man and animal lived intimately, a world where for the longest time, man saw himself as either on an equal footing with large prey animals or less powerful than they were. He knew they possessed a soul as he did. And when he killed them, their souls were yet there to be propitiated. Not only must they be killed properly, but after the kill there were rituals to be performed, right ways to treat the animal. The animal "must be given an opportunity of re-entry into life. This was the purpose of the earliest animal rites: the ritual interment of the skulls of the cave bear."[21]

It was Emil Bächler who excavated Drachenloch, one of the

caves I mentioned earlier. This cave was found at 8,000 feet above sea level and could not have been entered during the period of the Würm glaciation, which means that the remains in the cave had to be from 75,000 B.C. or earlier. In this cave (Bächler excavated two others in the region at slightly lower altitudes) he found flints, benches, work tables, and, as Joseph Campbell writes, "altars for the ritual of the bear—the earliest altars of any kind yet found, or known of, anywhere in the world."[22]

In the Drachenloch cave the bear skulls were found in the innermost part. One of them had a high bone pushed through between the cheekbone and upper skull. It is highly unlikely that this was the result of an accident, but it is particularly significant that the bear skulls were placed in the innermost part of the cave. This was true of subsequent Mousterian, or Middle Paleolithic, caves where the bear skulls were found in many other places.

"Leaping" ahead from 75,000 B.C. to Cro-Magnon man of the Upper Paleolithic, we find that now it is no longer just the animal remains that are in the caves, but also drawings and etchings of the animals—and in the very same innermost part of the cave. Here we come upon the fabulous paintings of Lascaux, Altamira, and many, many other sites.

The function of the caves and the cave paintings may never be known with certainty, yet we are necessarily driven to attempt a plausible answer, because it has so much to do with humanity. That care was taken to inter the bears' skulls seems certain. That in Cro-Magnon times great care and skill were expended on the paintings of the bear among other animals is also clear. But for what purpose? Or purposes? We are brought up short.

Some have suggested that through sympathetic magic, such a "ritual" might guarantee the future hunt. Others have suggested that paintings were somehow connected with a desire for the fertility (and thus greater numbers) of the animals, ensuring bounty. In the final chamber of Tuc d'Audoubert there are the relatively small heel marks of what have been described as younger men, perhaps around thirteen or fourteen, who had engaged in some kind of dance, perhaps a dance of initiation. Maybe it was within this inner sanctum that new members of this hunter society were taken into adult society and adult responsibility. The rites of this passage from adolescent to adult could have involved the sexual mysteries and concurrently (or at least in the same inner sanctum) the responsibilities of the hunt and of killing. And the responsibilities surely took into account the animal, the animal that had a soul, just like certain inanimate objects.

In tracking the cult of the bear northward out of central Europe to Finland and Asia, and onward into North America, we move again in great strides of time, though not as far as from Drachenloch to Tuc d'Audoubert. In the Finnish national epic of the *Kalevala,* we are on surer grounds as to the meaning of the bear and his treatment. The magic singer of the epic, Vainamoinen, kills the bear Otso and says: "Otso, thou my well-beloved, honey-eater of the woodlands, let not anger swell thy bosom; I have not the force to slay thee, willingly thy life thou givest as a sacrifice to Northland. Thou hast from the tree descended, glided from the aspen branches, slippery the trunks in autumn, in the fog-days, smooth the branches. . . . Leave thy cold and cheerless dwelling. . . . Come among the haunts of heroes, join thy friends in Kalevala. We shall never treat thee evil, thou shalt dwell in peace and plenty, thou shalt feed on milk and honey."[23] When the bear is brought home, he is told that he really has fallen down on his own, that he has been a willing victim.

In other stories of the people of northern Finland that are related to the killing of the bear, it is clear, as it is in the *Kalevala,* that the killing of an animal was not a trivial thing; and it was not a trivial matter *because* the animal had a soul and this soul needed propitiation.

The circumpolar bear cult finds its way across Siberia and ultimately to the Ainus of Japan, a seminomadic, Paleo-Siberian hunting and fishing people. Joseph Campbell, in a summary of the Ainus' ritual killing of the black bear, remarks that they have "the wonderful idea that the world of men is so much more beautiful than that of the gods that deities like to come here to pay us visits. On all such occasions they are in disguise."[24] The bear, the most divine visitor, is a mountain god (animals are not the only disguises of the gods, however; trees and even tools are gods).

If a very young bear cub is found, it is suckled by one of the women until it gets too rough. Then it is caged and fed for about two years. When the time comes to send the god back home, a festival is called. The man officiating says, "O Divine One, you were sent into this world for us to hunt. When you come to them, please speak well of us and tell them how kind we have been. Please come to us again and we shall again do you the honor of a sacrifice." At another part of the ceremony, some young men hold the bear, an arrow is shot into its heart, and he is strangled with two special sticks. He is skinned with his head still on, carried into the house, and offered food. Then he is told: "O Little Cub, we give you these prayer-sticks, dumplings, and dried fish; take them to your parents. Go straight to your parents without hanging about on your way, or some devils will snatch away the souvenirs. And when you arrive, say to your parents, 'I have been nourished for a long time by an Ainu father and mother and have been kept from all trouble and harm. Since I am now grown up, I have returned. And I have brought these prayer-sticks, cakes, and dried fish. Please rejoice!' If you say this to them, Little Cub, they will be very happy."[25] Then the flesh is eaten, while some of the men drink the blood, and finally the skull is placed upon a pole.

This same attitude of respect was to continue with the cult across the Bering land bridge into North America, on in fact to the western coast of this very Hudson Bay that we dwell on now. When Knud Rasmussen was on his way from Greenland to the western coast of Alaska on his famous Fifth Thule Expedition, he was to make friends with several shamans on his way west. No one was more interesting than Aua, of the Iglulik Eskimo on Hudson Bay, who explained to Rasmussen very poignantly this special relation that hunting people had with the forces of their world and how such forces were inescapable. "We fear the souls of dead human beings and of the animals we have killed." And his brother added: "The greatest peril of life lies in the fact that human food consists entirely of souls."[26] There, in the succinctest of statements, is the world of the hunter illuminated.

II

Three of our magic circle would leave us in the morning. Eric, as head of the Churchill detachment, felt he could not be away any longer, especially without radio contact. Jerry and Harry needed to catch the last of the twice-weekly flights to Winnipeg for their own obligations. Harry ran a one-man clinic, and his colleagues could only handle his big case load for a while. Too, Harry was rootless in a special way; and like the rootless, he needed to stay moving, in flux, until he found once more where he could rest. Who knows? Maybe, like the pelicans he so loved, he would keep circling until he could dive into marriage again.

Our bottles of magic potion were broken out once more. The ice from the fresh water ponds was cracked, aphids and all. In a sense there was a rootlessness for all of us here in the Muktuk, here on the tundra. Even for Len and Roy there was a sense of release from chores in Churchill—from the new Shell distributorship with people and planes needing fuel around the clock, and from the responsibilities of family.

For the rest of us there was the normal sense of release from one's own neighborhood, the kind that anyone feels while visiting a foreign country, for example. Whatever you wear, whatever fork you use, it's all right because you "don't know any better."

As many college students discover going to Europe, or vice versa, that can be an intoxicating rush.

For Eric, Jerry, and Harry (and Fred Treul), there was the release from occupation that is at the very root of *vacation*, from the Latin word *vacare*, which means "to be empty," "to be free." They could be "unoccupied" with their fairly weighty responsibilities back home. Besides the animals waiting on Harry, there were the people waiting on Eric and Jerry.

The week before we got to the little town of Churchill, an Indian woman had sneaked up to her boyfriend who was sleeping and drunk on the sofa, taken a long knife and stabbed him several times in the stomach. He had to be flown to Thompson, and she was awaiting trial. A couple of evenings later Eric and his wife Ardelle had been out for a brief stroll in the town after Eric was off work, when they saw in the gloom a man kicking violently what looked like a dog. Eric walked over (the man was also drunk) and discovered that it was another man, albeit small, who was huddled up in the gravel, by now unconscious. Eric had to manhandle the powerful villain and make him sit still, while he and Ardelle picked the gravel from the unconscious man's nose, mouth, and throat. For the briefest of times Eric was released from all this. To be safe among the bears, leaving the predators in town for the easier-to-understand predator of the ice.

For Jerry there would be the strangeness of going back to the Intelligence Section, where the news of the province-wide predation, pillage, and plunder would come streaming into this one place. But unlike some omniscient mind that might embrace the planet, this one only received the bad news. And that seems to be what we expect from each other in the twentieth century, particularly from such people as Eric and Jerry. For eight hours a day, we expect them to be prepared to kill someone who has already indicated he intends to kill them or others. We expect them to subdue violence with their bare hands if someone has gone berserk and doesn't have a gun; but we expect them at the same time to be subtle and skillful enough to stop the banker from embezzling the widow's mite, or to catch the pusher who will drop them for a sack of white powder. Then we want them to switch off all systems, return to wife and children, ask wife how day went (can't talk about their own), ask how children are, then join the principal pastime of Winnipeg parents during winter, which is taking the kids to hockey lessons or hockey games.

What astonishing pressures we put on the specialists of our age. And then we wonder why he or she cannot keep the ends in mind, cannot keep a balanced view. The skill of an ethical high-wire artist is required, but at unpredictable intervals one end of the wire is released.

Outside the wind was still blowing, but there was no snow. As the conversation touched on the weather, which it often did (would it be calm enough tomorrow for them to take off?), I think it was Bruemmer who brought up Vilhjalmur Stefansson, the anthropologist and explorer. One of Stefansson's book titles reflected his attitude about the Arctic: *The Friendly Arctic.* Rather than perpetuate the cliché of arctic *wastes,* he saw it more the way the Eskimos did, and then went even further. One of the main factors that limited arctic winter exploration was food. When an explorer reached the point where he had consumed half his food, he turned back. Stefansson said that not only explorers but Eskimos declared there was no animal life beyond their own frontiers, in what came to be called the "zone of inaccessibility" by explorers—meaning how far one could sled from where a ship had to stop, and still eat.

Stefansson felt otherwise and proved he was right. He was not shy about long expeditions. Several took five years each. Often he was thought to be dead because so much time passed before he would be heard from. But he learned to find seal under the ice far out on the frozen sea. He was thus able to go anywhere and live off the land—as long as he ate seal, as long as he did not lose his weapons, as long as he was not injured, as long as . . .

For his jaunts across the Arctic, like Rasmussen's somewhat later, patience was obviously a virtue much in demand. When bad weather caught up with the Eskimo, he often sat down with his back to the wind and waited . . . several days if necessary. Anyone traveling by air in the Arctic may have to wait for a week or two. It is much like dealing with the fog on the northwestern Pacific coast of Canada and the United States. Several weeks' wait is not uncommon.

One of the incongruities for me was to discover the popularity of American country music in the fastnesses of Canada. If I had thought more about the Prairie Provinces of the southwestern half of Canada, I might have been able to make the connection. Or had I remembered about the Calgary Stampede. Len had brought along a few tapes for his player, many of them country and western. With the departure of three of our members facing us, the voices of Charley Pride, Hank Williams, and Tom T. Hall, plus an ample toasting with the magic potion, helped to generate one of those rare transcendent moments. Even Harry, red suspenders and all, gave a demonstration of an Iowa farmer's idea of dancing. It appeared very much like a giant jack rabbit or kangaroo jumping in place with hands to the side, with an explanation that at some point he would take his lady fair around his shoulders and neck and continue spinning around, jumping in place all the time. The ethnologists of the Midwest should be alert to this.

At first the radio and tape player had been an unwelcome surprise for me. When one goes away from the town and the things of the town, he has the best chance to feel what has been lost by his living in a town. Unless he wants to do radical surgery on his civilized ways (including his twentieth-century tool kit), the attempt will always be a big compromise. He has become too unused to privation and discomfort for a sudden reentry into pure hunter, pure explorer. But bringing a radio and a tape player seemed to overthrow the very notion of the silent tundra (which

Stefansson has gone to great lengths to point out is not silent—almost never, whether through ice cracking, wind howling, summer loons and shore birds calling), the kind of experience you feel you need, to know you have been to such a place. Throughout the time I was with the crew of the Muktuk, I felt a persistent need to go out a mile or so away, to sit on a rock in the middle of the snow and let the whole white world stream in. For this I would have to wait until my summer return when the threat of coming upon a bear was less (though not gone). Once I realized the futility of fulfilling this desire, I began to do the exercise in my mind. It would never be the same; still it became a meditative triumph, an imaginative one, that permitted me to transport myself out from the magic circle, to the solitary point I would select, and open myself to the world's ebb and flow, even to the terror of the vastnesses like those one sometimes feels looking up at the stars.

Yet I could understand why we humans fall easily toward distractions, in the way a dog or bear will look to the side of your stare, uneasy with the being that seems to penetrate who it is. There is a violence in absolute, prolonged solitude, a deadly invasion. And the radio and recorded songs help to divert us from this uneasiness. When Knud Rasmussen first hit Canada in 1921 and ran into his first Canadian Eskimos, they had a party in a big snow hut, where the Eskimos danced to American country music on a gramophone! "The Eskimo men and women had learned, from the whalers, American country dances. Music was provided by the inevitable gramophone which seems to follow on the heels of the white man to most parts of the world. And the women were decked out in ball dresses hastily contrived for the occasion from material supplied by Captain Cleveland." Of course Rasmussen was disappointed in this kind of "corruption," because he was already too late in the early twentieth century to see the untouched Eskimo. Later, he met Igjugarjuk (the well-known shaman) and the Padlermiuts on the Barrens, expecting them to be living in a quite primitive state. But, he writes, "when a powerful gramophone struck up, and Caruso's mighty voice rang out from Igjugarjuk's tent, I felt that we had missed our market, as far as the study of these people was concerned. We were about a hundred years too late."

So the cleansing of silence aside, we had the white man's version of the Eskimo drum dance inside our "snow hut," and a way to bind with the beat of music, to unify perhaps for the reason that men have always beaten the drum or danced to the beat: a means of driving away the frightening spirits of stark boredom, the bad spirits of the great silence; or to call up the spirits so that the beat of the world may be gathered in a node of place, becoming a thing rather than a no-thing.

Finally Treul and Bruemmer made their way to the forward vehicle, their bunkmate Guravich long ago dead to the world. The others climbed into their bunks, and I turned down the wick of the lamp so only the barest of flickers still shone on the ice of the window, still threw shadows against the walls of sleeping men. I would soon roll into my own bunk, beneath the roped-in Harry (roped-in, because he didn't want to roll out of his top bunk, and certainly not while he had the drops in his eyes). But it had been my habit to sit up a bit longer than most for that sliver of solitude which I crave.

I did not doubt that many or all of the Muktuk were dreaming about bears. It is said that among the Omaha and Pawnees there were special bear societies. Only men who had had dreams involving bears were permitted, for these men were thought to have taken on the power of the animals. Like any men who are said to have special powers, these were admired and respected by some, feared by others. The Assiniboins, for whom one of the rivers that runs through Winnipeg is named, felt that the bear society members were as touchy and dangerous as the bears they dreamed of.

What powers were our members taking on? The hope of acquiring the power of endurance, a power and beauty forged under great pressure. There was that. But also we took on the knowledge of the vulnerability of even so great a power. This vulnerability reminded us of our own and maybe of the responsibility that the hunter has for the hunted.

As the flickering light danced the shadows in a phantasmagoria of shapes from the world of the known and the unknown, I continued to wonder how much I had in common with my brother of twenty thousand, even fifty thousand years ago. It remains surely to bring this "cult" of the bear forward from Aua and his brother to us who are gathered here to pay witness to the bear. What continuities, if any, are there? What meaning does the bear have for us as we lurch our way toward the end of the second millennium? Why have ten men, none of whom has any reputation as a spendthrift, spent what it took in money and time to get to this frozen world?

It is true that late twentieth-century North Americans are not bound to animals in the way Cro-Magnon man was, much less Neanderthal man. That seems an understatement. We are certainly not bound for our daily meals to the killing of wild animals. Up until very recently, the Eskimos were. The Padlermiuts (the Caribou Eskimos) were only evacuated to Eskimo Point from the Barrens as late as the 1950s. But there never were very many Eskimos, sixty thousand at a peak. The hundreds of millions of all the others in North America alone do not need wild land animals for food. What is true is that we are still bound to the killing of animals, but only special ones that we have found to be particularly to our taste. One might, though, include fish as wild animals we still pursue for serious food resources.

Yet the division of labor and the specialization of labor inherent in the very recent Industrial Age of some hundred years have fragmented and atomized our notion of process. It has been said many times, yet the truism remains, that many millions of people in large towns and cities do not associate their proxy killing of animals and the subsequent butchering as part of their lives; that the meat found in stores wrapped in plastic, looking very unlike a living animal, is for them divorced from the reality of organic process. This compartmentalization of experience has contributed to a ferociously narrow sense of existence. What is ironic is that this alienation from organic processes has resulted in new species of sentimentality about animals and about the processes upon which life rests. This tunnel vision resembles the understanding of a bunch of executives with offices atop some skyscraper, giving directions to those in the field. I remember a particular instance when men drilling an oil well in the Arctic radioed headquarters thousands of miles away that they needed to move their floating drilling rig immediately, a little earlier than anticipated, because the pack ice was going to do great damage. Headquarters radioed back that their "projections" demanded the rig remain. Disaster resulted, of course.

It is not incidental that one cannot very well arrive at a sacramental vision of the world if the perception of it is broken into discretenesses. And not only is there no interlocking of the visible and invisible as there likely was for Paleolithic man, but for most people today the animal has no soul. Thus, it does not have to be propitiated. Although it is not uncommon for modern men and women to talk to their domesticated animals, it is like talking to modern gods—there is no reply. Still we speak and ask questions of them. During our expedition, it was not uncommon for Guravich to lean out the window and address the bears.

Most people would say that the animal, including the bear, is no longer worshipped. And in any sense common to Paleolithic man that is likely true. In a way, however, for some, the animal, specifically the animals that look like us in some way, have been "re-throned." Why is this? I expect partly to retrieve our innocence, to make tracks back to Eden. In the face of what has been found east of Eden, there is an understandable desire for an about-face.

In the face of the terrifying fragmentedness of so much contemporary existence, returning to the world of the animal, or wilderness, is a way, our intuition tells us, to feel some sense of wholeness, to become part of some fabric of being. It is a retreat, in all of the senses of that word, to where elemental chores can assume their rightful preeminence: sleeping and eating; chopping wood to keep warm and to cook with; immersing oneself in sensory experience, as opposed to a chair-ridden "mentalness." And by these simplicities, we seek ultimately to feel more, to reduce the tool kits. Backpackers have the right idea. Thus, in a sense, the vestiges of the animal as an object of worship persist. And perhaps we still attempt to take on the power of animal, echoing much older times.

Perhaps many of our group would be loath to say they were trying to take on the power of the bear. Yet surely we can try to take on the bear's world imaginatively—always failing, but the better for attempting to, even knowing that we will fail. We can try to "put ourselves in his place." Through our imagination we are out on the ice with him, we wait with him as he lies in wait for the ringed seal, as he is followed by the arctic fox. We can be reminded of or reeducated to the nature of nature, of its perils if we should become temporarily insulated from the great fact of natural processes. We can be reminded, too, of the limits of the predator, especially us, the leading predator, Alpha of alphas. Part of that sense of limits is expressed in the intimacy of the stalker and the stalked, the slayer and the slain—and in the desperate need of the predator for the prey.

But what does this mean for us who get most of our life-sustaining food from the merely slain, the merely dead? After all, no one today needs the polar bear for food for the body. We need the idea of the bear, the bear's soul, in order to be able to run with him, that we may get as close as we can to running with the animals. And for this, we need his instruction. To watch his power in killing a seal, his swiftness in attack, is to be instructed still by the animal master. And to watch him as he kills a seal is to recall his great dependence on the seal, and ours on all the living world, plant and animal, that we need and devour.

The Muktuk, where we have gathered every night to talk about the beauty of the bear, his power, his majesty, reminds me of the small inner sanctum of sanctums in such Paleolithic caves as Tuc d'Audoubert. Where they had lamps of animal fat, we had a lamp of fossil fuel. Where the Old People needed to kill the bear, we did not. Yet they had live bear around them and at night, and we have them, many of them. Sometimes banging away at the sides of our fragile Muktuk perch, our plywood-sided cave of confessions, of ruminations about hunting and photography, Indians and Eskimos, tools like Len's machines and tools from Fred's foundries in Milwaukee. But always there was the bear. And his retinue of foxes and ravens and gulls.

The restricted space, the murkiness illuminated by the one small flame of light, served to compress the world. Concentrating the autonomous existence of all the men brought about not a loss of who we were, not a submerging, nor a homogeneity, but an intimacy of lives. That might have been different from any "ceremonies" or rites of passage that took place at Tuc d'Audoubert. There, a sublimation and submitting of the young men was desirable and useful. This wasn't what happened at Cape Churchill.

Or perhaps we did submit in our way. The awe and respect that we felt was, I think, partly the shared excitement of one predator watching another. The sudden speed and roar of a bear chasing an arctic fox, the guttural fierceness of one bear angry at another for whatever reason (over food, over a female) was exciting to us, brought our own blood up. Just as one's excitement over a hawk's or falcon's diving attack for prey, or over a hound chasing a fox or hare, is rooted in our predatory inheritance. (Even though these sensibilities may have been blunted by having proxy killers slay for us in abattoirs, and even making them, as they have been in Japan, an outcast or lower class.) There is simply a rush of the blood, of the adrenaline, in watching such an action. Add to that the respect and fear given an animal that can kill an unarmed man, can often kill a man armed only with a spear or a bow and arrow, can even kill a man with the wrong rifle or poor skill—all of that becomes a part of what we feel about the bear. Then surround our inner sanctum with a howling wind and the magic is there for those who would have it.

We can open ourselves to the bear's power so that he can touch us, touch us even beyond consciousness, and thereby we might be able to touch the world. We can try, must try. We can try and follow, even though we know we will fail, right at the veil of the ineffable, but a veil that blows and shifts in the winds of the mind and must be searched out in every present.

Throughout the millennia bears have been great shamans and teachers. Everyone knew that he must deal properly with the bear, like other animals and plants. For each had his spirit that must not be outraged, else he might bring down the world. The raven, that marvelous bird that was recognized early in history as the smart bird he was, appears frequently in creation stories. For the Bering Sea Eskimos he was the creator. After creating man and woman, and animals and plants for them to eat, he paused and surveyed what he had done in creating man. He then created the bear, because he felt that if he did not create something to make men afraid, they would destroy everything he had made to inhabit the earth.

Any beast or plant, having a spirit, could be a messenger of the mysteries, could come with a warning, could come as protector. Maybe that is part of the message of the bear for us—the very fact of his great size and power and yet his vulnerability, so dependent on seal from below and for his existence above from man. For if we permit the raven's warning through the bear to go unheeded, men may "destroy everything he had made to inhabit the earth." The bear can be the figure through which we can be transformed, can guide us as we try to bring our lives into accord with the life of the world. It is not a lack of scientific information, or the numbering of the world, that keeps us in such peril of plundering the planet and now perhaps of destroying everything that inhabits it. A transformation is what is needed, a transformation of attitude and spirit. Eskimos of today have noted that it has become increasingly difficult for men and animals to interchange forms. Maybe that's because as we have become so focused on the world of matter, organic and inorganic (and the objective investigations have been magnificent and fruitful), we have slipped into thinking that matter is all there is. And *strictly* speaking, the discrete provinces of animal ecology, or zoology, or botany, cannot and do not address whether, for example, we should eliminate or allow to be eliminated the polar bear, the carrier pigeon, or the pitcher plant. By making the animal or plant purely an object, we have somehow lost the unifying power of transformation, where one state of being changes into another. In physics, we overcame the object when we realized it was only an event in the transformation of energy. By being attentive and open to the world imaginatively, and by being obedient before the ultimate mystery of the world, we may be able to make the return to a single unifying energy, one wherein we can see ourselves as transformations within a single fabric or field—and thus son and brother of the bear.

I slipped on my coat and eased out on the deck, hanging on to the door in the wind so as not to wake the other members. The wind was free of snow and the stars were bright. At my feet stood the ghostly white outline of a huge male, waiting as if something was to happen, some prophecy that needed to be fulfilled. And streaming above and across the heavens was the aurora borealis. Great furlings of greens and yellows. Celestial drapery wisping in space like that curtain of the ineffable in the mind.

Perhaps one description of these high-speed charged particles from the sun is that they are striking our air molecules of oxygen and nitrogen, thus exciting or inducing them to luminosity. Samuel Hearne saw them too and noted in his journal, likewise in November, but in 1770, that the Chipewyans believed the northern lights were caused by a celestial deer having his fur rubbed and throwing off sparks just as his earthly counterpart would do if properly stroked.

Striding behind the streaming curtain was Ursa Major.

12

With three of our hardy band airlifted out, all of us could now squirm into the track vehicle. But since Len never wanted everyone to be in the same vehicle, in case one broke down, only six of the seven could abandon base camp. Either from anticipation of heavy freeze-up or just because they liked the terrain, what bears were left wanted to hang around a small island just a few hundred yards off the mainland. When no bears lounged around the Buggy this morning, off we went in pursuit, leaving Roy to man the Buggy (and giving him a rare chance for some solitude).

Everyone had 35 mm equipment, but Treul had also brought all his 2¼ × 2¼ format Hasselblad system. And I mean system. The longest telephoto screwed on looked like a small mortar. Guravich grumbled as if Treul were committing sacrilege by using the larger format. Treul did commit sacrilege by not being able to carry all his equipment alone. I often ended up being his camera-bearer.

All loaded, Len took off as if there were some urgency, and the relative speed magnified the bumps over the rocks. Hitting a smooth place in the ice, he hotdogged around, braking one track hard and spinning the whole bunch of us. Out on what would have been water, he picked his way more cautiously, not wanting to lose a track. Occasionally we were out of sight of Roy because of the lift and fall of the beaches. Once on the island we saw the skeleton of an old wooden boat. The only sign of former human life.

Often around late morning the bears seemed to nap. The bears at the Cape appeared to like the island for their morning siesta. In summertime, with no snow cover, these same bears dig down to the permafrost in order to cool off and also to avoid the flies that can be such a terror (and mosquitoes and no-see-ums!). It's like having air-conditioning always close at hand. The same permafrost is still used by some Indians and Eskimos for refrigeration. Just dig a deep hole and keep your meat and the hole covered. When I spent a summer on Herschel Island in the Beaufort Sea, a biologist friend of mine kept all his perishables in such an icebox for the entire summer, an icebox that had been used for perhaps a hundred years (or more) by Eskimos before him.

In winter, like now, day beds are dug in the snow by the bears for warmth and to get out of the wind. As we clanked by in our pint-sized panzer, suddenly first one pair of dark brown eyes peered from its bed, then another. Sometimes the sleeper would be solitary, other times as many as three napped together.

On the Bay side of the little island the circumstances were different. At first I thought one of our comrades was suffering from stomach discomfort, because a foul odor filled the vehicle. When someone remarked, "Uggh," I figured my suspicion was confirmed and pulled the plywood "sunroof" back to allow for some fresh air. Wrong! No fresh air there.

Bruemmer was laughing, because he knew what I had thought. We had entered a long stretch of kelp. What was left of the effects of tide (the ice was getting much thicker) was out, and the wide beds of kelp were everywhere. And even though it was well below freezing, what I was smelling was the familiar fragrance of "rotten eggs," or the results of anaerobic fermentation. The bears thought this was just dandy, however, and many preferred to dig their day beds in the kelp. Occasionally they would nibble on their kelp—sort of like having breakfast in bed, or breakfast *of* bed. Bears have been observed underwater diving to the bottom to nibble on kelp there.

As soon as we stopped to make pictures, we soon drew two curious bears, nap time or not. With the roof pulled back we could get shots from a lower angle than in the Buggy, but that meant we were closer to the bear's level. At first the two stood beside us and their heads were window level then. But finally they stood up with their front paws on the top. Their heads loomed above ours, even with us standing on the seats. We were taking chances, our sense of security heightened by their soft brown eyes, their cuddly look. One bear finally began to shake the light vehicle, just as others had done to the Muktuk Saloon. Part of the frame cracked and Len yelled, "Hey," as if the rules had been broken. He took a long straw broom and swatted the scrimmaging animal on the snout, whereupon the bear looked hurt and uncomprehending.

While we were lucky to stumble on such a bed of bears, still their numbers were dwindling. To the west of the island, back on the mainland, we hadn't seen any. They all seemed to be here on the island, like this was the final staging area, the closest they could get before launch.

We banged around for another hour, saw no new bears, and began to feel the pangs of hunger. All the chow was back in the Buggy.

13

Even though three more bunks were available in the Muktuk, the rituals had been established, so Bruemmer, Treul, and Guravich continued to sleep forward in the Buggy. With the Herr Panzerkommandant still turning in to get his full ten hours of sleep, the Muktuk continued long past his bedtime of squeaky clean underwear and socks. Correspondingly the Muktukers were not always ready to bound out of the bedrolls two hours before dawn, merely to be tantalized with Red River Cereal.

Thus it was that in the fog of half-sleep when we heard him trying to yell across through the Buggy door, the wind tunnel on the platform and the door of the Muktuk, we did what any self-respecting Muktuker would do. We rolled over in our sleeping bags, and dug in deeper. He kept calling for Len.

"Len! Len! It's a bear, Len!"

This was not the sort of announcement that was suited to bringing us out of the sack.

"Go back to bed," Len grumbled. Still the din from forward. Finally the door was flung open by this apparition in his long handles.

"Bring the gun, Len. Bring the gun. It's a bear." And the door slammed.

Still bitching, Len reached over the door and got the last weapon left on board, a 30.06, since the Mounties had gone with their heaters. The rest of us stayed in our sacks. This was simply someone crying bear too often.

Soon Len came back. "Christ, there was a bear. He tore off half of the front door." We all went racing forward, whereupon we had related to us the ursine comedy of the season.

Bruemmer slept all the way forward, then Guravich, then Treul. Bruemmer was awakened in the pitch dark of the Buggy by ripping sounds five feet away from his bunk. Finally as something went pop, he dug out his flashlight only to see this great white head above the driver's seat, with an arm inside too. He either threw the flashlight at the bear's head because that was the only weapon he had, or else it went out and he threw it in frustration and yelled a warning to Guravich. Guravich began yelling for Len, and the bear was trying to join the guys in the Buggy. (Remember: polar bears can't climb, right?) According to the testimony of his colleagues, Treul covered his head in his sleeping bag and made like a mummy. Len ripped off a couple of shots for effect and the uninvited guest eased back to the tundra.

This was how our final day began.

On the way back to Churchill we were mostly quiet, the fact of the impending break-up and departure much on our minds. Of course, the process had started with Harry, Eric, and Jerry. All of us were driven a little inward by that. Leaving our home on the Cape, however, made it final. There were the amenities of the town that we looked forward to, most especially our first shower, and a hot one at that, in two weeks. Yet with the return of each amenity, each luxury that we have become so accustomed to in our time, the more precious became the gathering, and perhaps the more elusive.

From this vortex spun out the new events, the new stories. Within one week of leaving Bruemmer in Winnipeg, I was to hear of his massive heart attack. We all realized, when we heard the news, that if Fred had had it on the Cape and not in Montreal, he wouldn't be with us now.

The next year the attempt was made again, but as might have been expected, it was a different experience. Five of the original band could not come. *Life* magazine came along, and this time we were being observed along with the bears. I am not sure we behaved with as much nonchalance as the bears. And at the end, just before another blizzard, Truel saw a beautiful and solitary ivory gull fly by. As he tried to take its picture, he leaned out a bit too far and an old bear standing underneath the vehicle took a big chunk out of his arm. He nearly bled to death before he could be gotten in to the doctors. Bruemmer had another heart attack during the year. (He no longer carries cigarettes for Len to bum.)

I remember that as we neared town a large raven stood on a rock. He seemed to cock his head in irony.

14

On the way out to catch the plane to Winnipeg, I was to stop off at what is known as D-20, the number stenciled onto an old building used as a holding facility for the bears. These are the bears that are not content with their fellows out on the Cape, or even further north. Some may have visited Churchill for the first time; others are old friends. Records suggest that the cubs of a mother who frequents the garbage dump several miles out of Churchill are also likely to become "dump bears."

Occasionally a bear will wander around town and become a possible source of danger for the schoolchildren, or for those who insist on wandering about late at night. The Mounties and the Wildlife Service people either try to drive them away with thunder-flashes, or if the noise won't work, dart them with PCP, the drug known on the street as "angel dust." (Subsequently, because there was danger of the drug falling into the hands of users, another drug was chosen for this purpose.) The bears are then hauled to the holding facility to await freeze-up when they prefer seal to garbage.

D-20 was at capacity when I entered the arched building of the Quonset hut. They were going to try again today to anesthetize one of the boarders and take him by helicopter a few miles out on the ice. Just on the right, as you first entered, was a large cage where a bear lay on a big stretcher, on his stomach. His tongue flopped outside his mouth. One of the workers was taking his temperature rectally. As the worker walked to the front, he clapped his hands lightly and moved one hand in front of the bear's face to test for any reaction. The eyes managed to flicker. Some salve was placed on the eyes to protect them, because when a bear is under the influence of this drug, his eyes will not close. The pulse is checked. Someone explained to me that the pulse rate was only three per minute, another side effect of the drug.

We moved on down the line of cages toward a bear that was going to be doped. As the worker loaded the syringe that was attached to a long tube, the bear growled. He had been shot yesterday, but could not be coptered out because the wind had been too strong. He made the mistake of turning his rear toward where we were and got shot again. He paced rapidly around his cage very briefly, but just as rapidly began to show signs of stumbling and awkwardness. Then he was down. But the guy didn't open the door immediately. He waited just a bit, then jabbed the bear several times with a stick. No response. He drew his revolver and opened the cage door easily. All of us felt the tension. I was glad to be outside. Easing the revolver back but with the strap still off, the worker clapped his hands, then yelled. Suddenly there was a roar and the color drained from his ruddy face. I mean right then. But it was the bear in the next cage. We all relaxed and he checked the pulse, seeming to minister tenderly to his patient.

Outside we could hear the thump-thump-thump of the chopper settling down next to the building. We moved back to the bear on the stretcher. The larger cage was opened and the stretcher was dragged outside. Spread out on the ground was a large net like the ones used to load cargo ships. The nine hundred pounds of great white bear were eased onto the net, his paws and head carefully adjusted for the most comfortable ride. The ends of the thick net were secured, and then this was secured to the line to the chopper. Although the bear could have been lifted yesterday in the strong winds, what can happen is that the nine hundred pounds below can begin to swing in wider and wider arcs, jerking the machine about and perhaps out of the sky.

We stood back, shielding our eyes from the dust and pebbles thrown up by the blades, and partly against the sun. The machine and the bear ascended for several hundred feet and paused a moment, as if to test the wind. Just at that moment I was reminded of that scene in the Fellini film where the helicopter is moving across the city of Rome, a giant statue of Jesus held suspended below, resurrected. As if assured, our own chopper now headed toward the east and the frozen Bay.

Lords

I

Nose high over the ice rim
He was. No sound in the arctic morning,
Moving as if the whole white world
Were his, a majesty of generations.
The slight northern sun
Let the bear's aura flame out
As he trudged the jagged ice
Toward us on our guarded perch;
We had come to behold the white lord.

Like any god he would devour us
Were we not beyond his reach.
Yet we leaned toward him,
As close as his breath.
(How tantalizing, the black lips!)
Staring now at the great head,
Now into the hot opaque brown eyes
We plumb the heart of wildness
In a cold white land.

Some among us come not only for awe;
Some come to measure,
To send reports to that place
Where all numbers are gathered.

Not satisfied with the simple telemetry of grandeur,
They want to know wherefore the lord,
How and how much.

II

Abrupting across the silent land
The helicopter whirls low
Bearing these curious men
Who mean to leave no mystery unturned.

Swooping, the swirling bird
Unleashes its dose of angel dust,
Hovers—while the lord stumbles and falls—
Then lights near the body.
The inquisitive come out,
Guns drawn in the pale light.

III

Prostrate before you,
Every orifice violated,
You learn my heat,
My breath strokes, my age.
I cannot close my eyes
Before what you do.

As long as you have known yourself as man
You have tried to put on my power,
My head on your own head
In skull-lined caves across the world.

You try to take it on now
By numbering each piece of this world,
And in a distant moment
To hold all pieces in mind,
To be done
With the stink and stature of bear.

IV

You step back
As I begin to move.
You gather in groups for life's only reason,
To bring the big animal down.

But I must be kept alive,
Who know cold as you have never known it,
Who even taught The People how to hunt.

Without me you walk in deserts.
Imprison me, you cage yourselves.

Again now up from within myself,
Up from the gulag of limits
To the pure white dream.

Bounding the eskers fingering the sea
I go to meet the seal to be killed,
Who awaits me like a lover.

Rising up from this sleep
I assume myself.

I move out among the toothed sea rocks
Of the receded tide,
The frozen rocks like flowers.
Whale killer, strider of ice,
The Alpha of my retinue
Of foxes, ravens, and gulls, and
Now you who need me too.
We die, we devour each other,
We live to die again.

Notes

1. Miller Williams, "Euglena," *Halfway from Hoxie, New and Selected Poems* (Baton Rouge: LSU Press, 1977), 34. Reprinted by permission of the author.

2. Wallace Stevens, "Sunday Morning," *The Collected Poems of Wallace Stevens* (New York: Alfred A. Knopf, Inc., 1954), 69–70. Copyright © 1923, renewed 1951, by Wallace Stevens. Reprinted by permission of Random House, Inc., and Alfred A. Knopf, Inc.

3. Susan Sontag, *On Photography* (New York: Dell Publishing Co., 1973), 23.

4. *Ibid.*

5. *Ibid.,* 155

6. *Ibid.,* 155, 161.

7. *Ibid.,* 23.

8. Gordon Speck, *Samuel Hearne and the Northwest Passage* (Caldwell, Idaho: Caxton Printers, Ltd., 1963), 129.

9. Wallace Stevens, "Anecdote of a Jar," *Collected Poems,* 76. Copyright © 1923, renewed 1951, by Wallace Stevens. Reprinted by permission of Random House, Inc., and Alfred A. Knopf, Inc.

10. C. C. A. Gosch, ed., *Danish Arctic Expeditions, 1605 to 1620: Book II, The Expedition of Captain Jens Munk to Hudson's Bay in Search of a North-West Passage in 1619–20* (London: Hakluyt Society, 1907), 24–25.

11. *Ibid.,* 31.

12. José Ortega y Gasset, *Meditations on Hunting,* trans. Howard B. Westcoll, with an introduction by Paul Shepard (New York: Scribners, 1972), 106–107.

13. *Ibid.,* 108.

14. *Ibid.,* 12.

15. *Ibid.,* 12–13.

16. *Ibid.,* 57.

17. *Ibid.,* 109.

18. S. Giedion, *The Eternal Present: The Beginnings of Art* (New York: Pantheon Books, 1962), 278.

19. *Ibid.,* 282, quoting Freud.

20. *Ibid.,* 284.

21. *Ibid.,* 285.

22. Joseph Campbell, *The Masks of God: Primitive Mythology* (London: Viking Press, 1959). All page references to this title cite the 1976 Penguin Books edition. 341.

23. Giedion, *The Eternal Present,* 288–89.

24. Campbell, *The Masks of God: Primitive Mythology,* 335.

25. *Ibid.,* 337.

26. Knud Rasmussen, *Report of the Fifth Thule Expedition, 1921–24* (Copenhagen: Gyldendaske Boghandel, Nordisk Forlag, 1930), vol. VII, nos. 1 and 2, 56.